Oracle Enterprise Manager 12c Command-Line Interface

Kellyn Pot'Vin

Seth Miller

Ray Smith

Apress®

Oracle Enterprise Manager 12c Command-Line Interface

ISBN-13 (pbk): 978-1-4842-0239-5

ISBN-13 (electronic): 978-1-4842-0238-8

Managing Director: Welmoed Spahr
Lead Editor: Jonathan Gennick
Developmental Editor: James Markham
Technical Reviewer: Hans Forbrich and Sarah Brydon
Editorial Board: Steve Anglin, Mark Beckner, Ewan Buckingham, Gary Cornell, Louise Corrigan, Jim DeWolf, Jonathan Gennick, Robert Hutchinson, Michelle Lowman, James Markham, Matthew Moodie, Jeff Olson, Jeffrey Pepper, Douglas Pundick, Ben Renow-Clarke, Dominic Shakeshaft, Gwenan Spearing, Matt Wade, Steve Weiss
Coordinating Editor: Jill Balzano
Copy Editor: April Rondeau
Compositor: SPi Global
Indexer: SPi Global
Artist: SPi Global
Cover Designer: Anna Ishchenko

Distributed to the book trade worldwide by Springer Science+Business Media New York, 233 Spring Street, 6th Floor, New York, NY 10013. Phone 1-800-SPRINGER, fax (201) 348-4505, e-mail orders-ny@springer-sbm.com, or visit www.springeronline.com. Apress Media, LLC is a California LLC and the sole member (owner) is Springer Science + Business Media Finance Inc (SSBM Finance Inc). SSBM Finance Inc is a Delaware corporation.

For information on translations, please e-mail rights@apress.com, or visit www.apress.com.

Apress and friends of ED books may be purchased in bulk for academic, corporate, or promotional use. eBook versions and licenses are also available for most titles. For more information, reference our Special Bulk Sales–eBook Licensing web page at www.apress.com/bulk-sales.

Any source code or other supplementary material referenced by the author in this text is available to readers at www.apress.com. For detailed information about how to locate your book's source code, go to www.apress.com/source-code/.

I dedicate this book to my children, Sam, Cait, and Josh, who are my reason for setting an example every day of my life.

—Kellyn Pot'Vin-Gorman

I dedicate this book to my fellow authors: Kellyn for providing me much needed guidance on my first journey as a book author, and Ray for his encouragement and just the right amount of persistence.

—Seth Miller

I dedicate this book to all the volunteers and staff at IOUG. Thanks for helping me become a better technologist and a much better person.

—Ray Smith

Contents at a Glance

Contents

About the Authors

Kellyn Pot'Vin-Gorman is an Oak Table Network Member. She was an Oracle ACE Director until joining Oracle as the Consulting Member for the Strategic Customer Program, a specialized group of Enterprise Manager specialists. She specializes in environment optimization tuning, automation, and creating systems that are robust and at the Enterprise level. Kellyn works almost exclusively on mult-TB-size databases, including Exadata and solid-state disk solutions and is known for her extensive work with both the Enterprise Manager 12c and its command-line interface. Her blog, `http://dbakevlar.com`, along with her social media activity under her handle, **DBAKevlar**, is well respected for its insight and content. She is the co-author of a number of technical books, hosts webinars for ODTUG, OTN, and All Things Oracle, and has presented at Oracle Open World, HotSos, Collaborate, and KSCOPE, along with numerous other U.S. and European conferences. Kellyn is a strong advocate for Women in Technology (WIT), citing both education on topics such as stereotypes and the presentation of early opportunities as being part of the path to overcoming challenges.

Seth Miller is an Oracle ACE and has been working with Oracle technologies since 2005. He has worked as a DBA in a number of industries, including health care, medical device manufacturing, and environmental science, and he now works as a consultant and an Oracle University Certified Instructor. Seth is a strong advocate for Oracle products and the Oracle community, serving as the IOUG Director of Volunteer Engagement, serving as the Vice President of the Twin Cities Oracle Users Group, engaging in social media conversations concerning Oracle technology, and participating in discussions on the Oracle-L mailing list. Seth is a regular speaker at the IOUG Collaborate and Oracle OpenWorld conferences, as well as a host of webinars for OTN. His blog, `http://sethmiller.org`, features posts related to Oracle and other technology. Enterprise Manager has found a special place in Seth's heart as a means of lightening the load of the IT administrator, while at the same time empowering them.

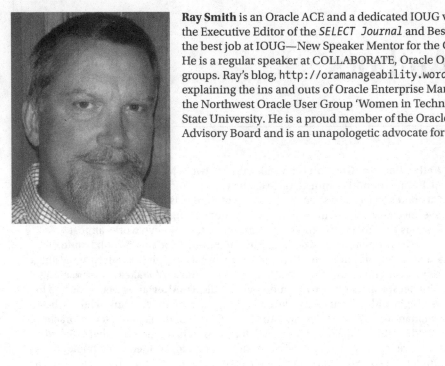

Ray Smith is an Oracle ACE and a dedicated IOUG volunteer. He currently serves as the Executive Editor of the *SELECT Journal* and Best Practices booklet, along with the best job at IOUG—New Speaker Mentor for the COLLABORATE Conference. He is a regular speaker at COLLABORATE, Oracle Open World, and at regional user groups. Ray's blog, `http://oramanageability.wordpress.com`, is dedicated to explaining the ins and outs of Oracle Enterprise Manager. He recently established the Northwest Oracle User Group 'Women in Technology' scholarship at Portland State University. He is a proud member of the Oracle Enterprise Manager Customer Advisory Board and is an unapologetic advocate for OEM.

About the Technical Reviewers

Oracle ACE Director and Electrical Engineer **Hans Forbrich** has been using Oracle technologies since 1984. During the 1990s, Hans gained considerable experience working with, and for, Oracle in the telecommunications industry across North America. He left Oracle at the end of 2002 to start Forbrich Consulting Ltd., a private company specializing in leveraging Oracle licenses through intelligent architecture, administration, and training. In his practice, Hans has used the Oracle Enterprise Manager family of products, which he has done since their inception in the early Oracle 8 time frame.

Hans has been happily married for over 30 years and has three adult children. In his "spare" time, Hans enjoys the arts with his wife, Susanne, and is a member of the Edmonton Opera Chorus.

Sarah Brydon is an accomplished technologist with more than two decades of experience with Oracle and UNIX based applications. An Oracle DBA since 1996, Sarah has worked with all versions of Oracle from 7.1 and is an Oracle Certified Master. She has extensive experience in system design and support for 24x7 environments, in Oracle RAC deployments and in security and audit considerations for Oracle databases.

Previously Sarah was a Senior Oracle Specialist for Blackrock, the largest global financial services company with more than 3 trillion dollars in assets under management. Sarah is currently a Senior Member of Technical Staff (Database Engineering) at Paypal.

Acknowledgments

I thank my husband, Tim Gorman, the best partner anyone could ask for and the Oracle community for their continued support and quest for knowledge.

My wife, Katie, brings order to my life, and my two children, Isaac and Adalyn, share their immeasurable joy with me every day. I'd like to thank the Oracle community for their amazing capacity to always make me want to be a better technologist.

My wife, Valerie, makes my life better every day. Her encouragement for this project was essential to its completion. I'd also like to thank the tremendous Oracle employees responsible for making OEM the fine tool that it is. Werner De Gruyter, Ana McCollum, Adeesh Fulay, and Maureen Byrne have all shown a genuine interest in improving OEM through user feedback and understanding. Their insights brought all of this into focus.

## CHAPTER 1

Architecture

Oracle Enterprise Manager 12c provides a scalable and reliable central repository, a console, and services for managing your all of your Oracle products. Users typically interact with OEM through the OEM console, which has a rich intuitive graphical interface.

The Enterprise Manager Command-Line Interface (EM CLI) provides access to OEM system functionality outside of the console. Interactive EM CLI tasks can replace lengthy click-streams in defining EM administrator accounts and roles, as one example of its usefulness. EM CLI interactive commands can be used in shell scripts or can be CLI invoked through CLI's own scripting mode in Jython.

This book explores different ways you can apply these techniques to simplify and automate tasks in your Oracle environment.

Enterprise Manager Framework

The Oracle Enterprise Manager application runs as a JEE application in a WebLogic Server J2EE domain on a WebLogic server. This combination is known as the Oracle Management Server, or OMS.

Java processes running on the OMS gather and process XML file uploads that come from EM agents on your remote hosts. That information is posted to a repository database, where it is stored in the SYSMAN schema.

When you view a page on your OEM console, the data is assembled from the repository database for presentation. In the same way, commands that you issue from the console are processed through the OMS to update repository information (metric collection or notifications, for instance) or manipulate managed targets either through a call to the EM agent or through an authenticated connection to a remote database or host.

Each command issued by the console executes a Java program. The console solicits and assembles data as well as the input commands required for those routines to execute. Much of the manipulative and query code base can be accessed through EM CLI.

The EM CLI program is itself a lightweight Java program that performs the same activities as the console pages but runs an immediate execution of OMS modules using values passed as command-line inputs; it is often employed in shell scripts or Jython programs.

EM CLI Verbs

Interface commands are referred to as *verbs*. Each verb performs a single task and either succeeds with reasonable feedback or comes back with a quick and obvious failure message.

Many verbs require input values on the command line. As with a PL/SQL package, your input must be passed to the OMS using very specific syntax. The values are always preceded by a filter keyword, and most input requires your strings to be wrapped in double-quotes.

■ **Note** The authors' experiences using quotation marks have been mixed. They are recommended, but often aren't required. We'll use them for clarity in our examples. You may find that you don't always need them, or that you prefer not to use them.

Use the get_targets verb to display or capture a list of the targets in your environment, as follows:

```
emcli get_targets
```

To find only Oracle database targets you'd filter your request with the targets keyword:

```
emcli get_targets -targets="oracle_database"
```

Numerous examples throughout this book demonstrate how verbs and input values are applied. A catalog of EM CLI verbs and their syntax is available in Oracle Support document E17786-x. Be aware that some verbs are tied to management packs that require licensing fees. You can also find online help at the command-line that lists all of the verbs available and their intended use. For example:

```
emcli help
Summary of commands:

    argfile     -- Execute emcli verbs from a file
    help        -- Get help for emcli verbs (Usage: emcli help [verb_name])
    login       -- Login to the EM Management Server (OMS)
    logout      -- Logout from the EM Management Server
    setup       -- Setup emcli to work with an EM Management Server
    status      -- List emcli configuration details
    sync        -- Synchronize with the EM Management Server
    version     -- List emcli verb versions or the emcli client version

  Add Host Verbs
    continue_add_host           -- Continue a failed Add Host session
    get_add_host_status         -- Displays the latest status of an Add Host session.
    list_add_host_platforms     -- Lists the platforms on which the Add Host operation
                                   can be performed.
    list_add_host_sessions      -- Lists all the Add Host sessions.
    retry_add_host              -- Retry a failed Add Host session
    submit_add_host             -- Submits an Add Host session.
...
```

The help verb can be filtered with specific verbs to display detailed usage instructions:

```
emcli help get_targets
  emcli get_targets
        [-targets="[name1:]type1;[name2:]type2;..."]
        [-alerts]
        [-noheader]
        [-script | -format=
                        [name:<pretty|script|csv>];
                        [column_separator:"column_sep_string"];
                        [row_separator:"row_sep_string"];
        ]
```

```
     [-config_search="Configuration Search UI Name"]
     [-unmanaged]
```

Description:
  Obtain status and alert information for targets.

Options:
  -targets=name:type
      Name or type can be either a full value or a pattern match
      using "%". Also, name is optional, so the type may be
      specified alone.
   -config_search="Configuration Search UI Name"
      Search UI Name should be the display name of the configuration search.
  -alerts
      Shows the count of critical and warning alerts for each target.
  -noheader
      Display tabular output without column headers.
  -script
      This option is equivalent to -format="name:script".
  -format
      Format specification (default is -format="name:pretty").
      -format="name:pretty" prints the output table
         in a readable format but is not intended to be parsed by scripts.
      -format="name:script" sets the default column separator
         to a tab and the default row separator to a newline.
         The column and row separator strings may be specified
         to change these defaults.
      -format="name:csv" sets the column separator to a comma
         and the row separator to a newline.
  -unmanaged
      Get unmanaged targets (no status or alert information)

Output columns:
    Status ID Status Target Type Target Name Critical Warning

Examples:
  emcli get_targets
      Shows all targets. Critical and Warning columns are not shown.

  emcli get_targets
      -alerts
      Shows all targets. Critical and Warning columns are shown.

  emcli get_targets
      -targets="oracle_database"
      Shows all "oracle_database" targets.

  emcli get_targets
      -targets="%oracle%"
      Shows all targets whose type contains the string "oracle".

```
emcli get_targets
      -targets="database%:%oracle%"
  Shows all targets whose name starts with "database" and type
  contains "oracle".

emcli get_targets
      -targets="database3:oracle_database"
      -alerts
  Shows status and alert information on the Oracle database named
  "database3".

emcli get_targets
      -config_search="Search File Systems on Hosts"
      -targets="oracle%:host"
      -alerts
  Shows status and alert information of the resulting targets from
  configuration search named "Search File Systems on Hosts" and targets
  whose name starts with "oracle" and of type "host".

emcli get_targets
      -targets="host"
      -unmanaged
  Shows name and type information for unmanaged host targets.
```

EM CLI Client Software

The basic OEM installation on a management server preconfigures an EM CLI client as part of OMS Oracle Home. In Chapter 2 we'll show you how to upgrade that client to the EM CLI Advanced Kit.

Part of EM CLI's strength comes from its flexibility. In addition to the client installation on the OMS server, you can install the EM CLI client on a non-OMS host or even on your desktop.

Installing the EM CLI client consists of downloading and extracting an installation jar file in order to install the binaries, and then configuring the client with connection information for your OMS server. The jar file and installation for its use are available through the OEM console under *Setup > Command-Line Interface*. Follow the instructions on that web page to install the EM CLI to your workstation.

EM CLI and EMCTL

Several EM CLI functions can be performed through the Agent Control utility EMCTL. Your choice of technique depends on a combination of factors.

- EM CLI client must be manually installed and maintained on the remote host when called by shell scripts on the remote host. The console displays a listing of remote CLI client installations, but you still have to manually update the client software.

- EM CLI configuration on a remote host requires connection information for interaction with the OMS server. When this information changes, you must visit each EM CLI installation.

- EMCTL commands are specific to the targets known to a specific agent, so the commands passed on the command line are typically much simpler.

- You must be logged in on the remote host to execute an EMCTL command. EM CLI allows you to perform many EMCTL-equivalent commands remotely in order to avoid a trip to the server. This can be particularly helpful when managing a number of servers in one session.

We recommend using EMCTL when you're just getting started or if your installation is small. Commands in EMCTL tend to be simpler, and the setup ahead of time is also simpler. The "investment" in time to get set up using EM CLI however, becomes worthwhile at scale. Those with large infrastructures to support will find themselves tending toward using EM CLI.

Agent Start and Stop

EM agents can be started and stopped from inside the OEM console, through EM CLI, and of course by EMCTL. Since EMCTL commands are performed for a single agent, the commands tend to be quite simple:

```
emctl start agent
```

```
emctl stop agent
```

Similar functionality can be performed from the management server, your desktop, or any host with the EM CLI client installed. Portability comes with complexity since you have to identify not only the agent to be controlled, but also the credentials to be used.

You can specify a host user, a named credential, or a credential set. When you pass the username you also have to provide a password. In a purely interactive mode you can be prompted for the password, but using this technique in a shell script may expose the password to other operating system users. Using OEM named credentials avoids this issue:

```
emcli start_agent -agent_name="dbservera:3872" -host_username="oracle" -host_pwd="Souper_53cre3t"
emcli start_agent -agent_name="dbservera:3872" -credential_name="oraprod"
emcli start_agent -agent_name="dbservera:3872" -credential_setname="HostCreds"
```

The stop commands require the same conditional values; for instance:

```
emcli stop_agent -agent_name="dbservera:3872" -host_username="oracle"
```

We'll explore some of these options in greater depth in Chapter 4.

Centralization

Perhaps you've decided to shut down some of your EM agents during a physical server move or perhaps during operating system patching. You can quickly build a list of the affected agents with EM CLI get_targets for oracle_emd types and turn that list into two CLI argfiles—one to stop the agents and another to start them.

■ **Note** Argfiles are used to process batches of CLI commands. They are discussed in more detail in Chapter 5.

Following is an example putting argfiles to use:

```
touch argfile_stop.lst
touch argfile_start.lst
emcli get_targets | grep oracle_emd > workfile.lst
for thisAGENT in `cat workfile.lst`; do
        echo "start_agent -agent_name=${thisAGENT} -credential_name=oraprod" > argfile_start.lst
        echo "stop_agent -agent_name=${thisAGENT} -credential_name=oraprod" > argfile_stop.lst
done
```

```
emcli login -user="SYSMAN"
emcli sync
emcli argfile ./argfile_stop.lst
logout
```

Access

Larger Oracle environments may have a separation of duties between the OEM administrator and regular DBA staff, or perhaps your security rules make it difficult to visit servers for routine maintenance. In those cases, running the CLI commands or managing up/down through the console makes sense.

Safety Net

You are prompted for a confirmation any time you ask to perform a dangerous task in the OEM console. EM CLI doesn't have the same functionality. When you give a command your task is executed exactly as you requested, so be mindful when deleting or modifying targets. Despite this, many people prefer the command line for its direct actions without excess feedback. Just be careful.

■ ■ ■

## CHAPTER 2

Installation and Security Framework and EM12c Release 4

Now that you understand the Enterprise Manager architecture, you may want to understand more-advanced installation methods for the Oracle Management Service (OMS) host or for a remote installation. You'll also want to be up to date on the latest verbs that come into play with 12.1.0.4, also known as EM12c Release 4, which is all covered in this chapter.

EM CLI and WebLogic Installation

Enterprise Manager runs as a domain on a WebLogic server (WLS). The cloud life-cycle solution couldn't exist without the middle-tier architecture provided by WebLogic. WLS handles the business logic along with communicating with web services and other remote processing to ensure front-end transactions are completed from beginning to end.

There was a time when the OMS required a separate installation of the WLS. Although it's currently an automated step in the installation of EM12c, comprehending how to perform this manually is valuable to the administrator, especially going forward when administering and managing the environment.

The WebLogic server must be made available to and synchronized with the Enterprise Manager Command-Line Interface (EM CLI) in order to offer the latest plug-ins, management packs, and full access to the Enterprise Manager Cloud environment.

Requirements

In order to understand the requirements before the EM CLI installation on your OMS proceeds, ensure that the WebLogic Domain Provisioning Profile is created in such a way that the software library has the Middleware Home that belongs to the domain archived and stored as part of the WebLogic domain.

Creating the WebLogic Domain Provisioning Profile

There are three components that make up the provisioning profile:

- a middleware home
- the binaries used by the WebLogic server components
- the domain configuration for the provisioning profile

If you simply have an administrator or super administrator log in to the EM12c environment, it will not be sufficient to complete the WLS domain provisioning profile. To complete this task, you must have the following:

- Host credentials for the WLS and any other host involved in the provisioning setup. These credentials were required during the initial OEM installation.

- All targets must have Java Required Files (JRF) enabled, which is discovered and monitored by Enterprise ManagerEnsure.

Log in to the Enterprise Manager Cloud Console as a super user and click on Enterprise, Provisioning and Patching, and then Software Library, as shown in Figure 2-1.

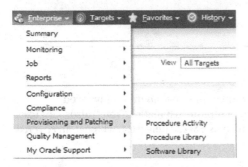

Figure 2-1. *Accessing the software library within the EM12c console*

Once you enter the software library, you will need to create a folder in which to store the profile (Figure 2-2).

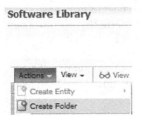

Figure 2-2. *Creating a new folder within the software library for provisioning, patching, or installations*

The Software Library already has a pre-determined set of sub-directories available. For our example, we will create a new directory named Profile_Home, give a defined description, and save it to a newly defined Networks sub-directory (Figure 2-3).

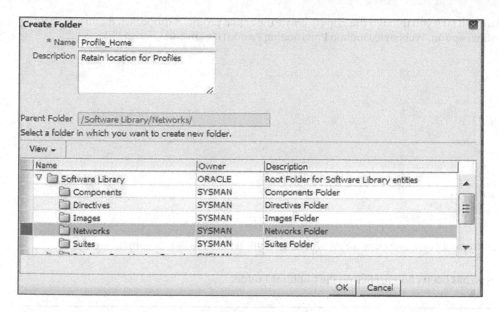

Figure 2-3. *Creation and details for the Profile_Home folder to be used for the WebLogic EM CLI installation*

Once satisfied with the entries, click OK. You will be shown that the directory was created successfully as well as the location of the new sub-directory off the software library directory tree (Figure 2-4).

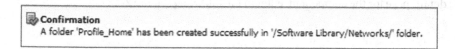

Figure 2-4. *Confirmation of successful folder creation in the software library within the Networks directory*

You will be returned to the software library main menu. Once more, click Actions, Create Entity, and then Component (Figure 2-5).

Figure 2-5. *The Actions menu, displaying expanded options to access the component-creation action in the software library*

The component wizard will take you through the steps to create the actual profile. A dropdown menu will show on the screen; choose the final option, WebLogic Domain Provisioning Profile (Figure 2-6).

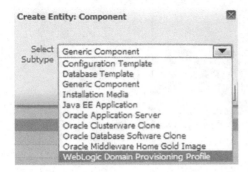

Figure 2-6. *Creating an entity for a WebLogic Domain Provisioning Profile within the EM12c console*

Once the profile subtype has been chosen, click on the Continue button.

___

■ **Note**   Don't be concerned if it takes a bit of time before the next step in the process returns to the screen. There is a delay at the Continue step.

___

Once the wizard arrives at the details page for the component, enter in the following (Figure 2-7):

- Name

- Description

- Other attributes (these settings can also be set on the home page for your WebLogic server)

Create WebLogic Domain Provisioning Profile : Describe

Parent Directory Profile_Home
            Subtype WebLogic Domain Provisioning Profile

Specify name, description and other attributes that describe the entity. These attributes are shared by all revisions of this entity. Additionally, attach any documents and keep notes.

* Name WL_Profile_EM1
Description Weblogic Provisioning Profile

Other Attributes

Name	Value
PRODUCT_VERSION	12.3.4
PRODUCT	Weblogic Domain
VENDOR	Oracle

Figure 2-7. *Filling out description and values for a new WebLogic Domain Provisioning Profile*

Don't add any file attachments or any other information, but simply click Next. You will then be asked about selecting a WebLogic service. Before choosing one, ensure that the box is checked for "Include the binaries for the Middleware Home in the profile to be created." This is essential for the profile to be created correctly.

Click on the magnifying glass next to "No WebLogic Domain Selected." A pop-up will show available WebLogic domains (Figure 2-8).

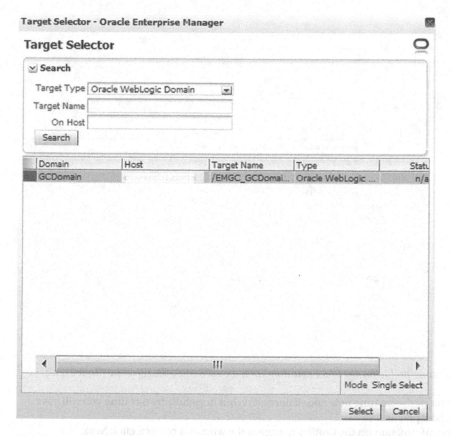

Figure 2-8. *Selecting a target to add to the WebLogic domain in the EM12c console*

You can simplify the search, but most environments have only a few WebLogic servers. Choose the one that you wish to use from the list and click Select.

The Configure page will require you to review the data you've chosen so far (Figure 2-9). Correctly set a working directory that exists and has at least 200 MB of free space for work files. If you set the working directory incorrectly or if there is not enough space, the job will fail, which will leave profile components to be cleaned up and recreated from the beginning of this step. This also is in no way your final storage location for your profile, and all working files will be cleaned up after processing.

Create WebLogic Domain Provisioning Profile : Configure

Parent Directory Profile_Home
Subtype WebLogic Domain Provisioning Profile

☑ Include the binaries from the Middleware Home in the profile to be created.

WebLogic Domain GCDomain 🔍

Host emrep1.oral.com

* Working Directory /tmp/fmwProvSrc

⌄ **Source Information**

Component	Location
▽ 🖥️GCDomain	/u01/app/oracle/product/oms12c/gc_inst/user_projects/domains/GCDomain
▽ 🗀Middleware Home	/u01/app/oracle/product/oms12c
🖥️ WebLogic Server 10.3	/u01/app/oracle/product/oms12c/wlserver_10.3
▽ 🗀Oracle Home(s)	
🖥️oms	/u01/app/oracle/product/oms12c/oms
🖥️Oracle_WT	/u01/app/oracle/product/oms12c/Oracle_WT

⌄ **Host Credentials**

Select credential from one of the following options.

Credential ⦿ Preferred ◯ Named ◯ New
Preferred Credential Name [Normal Host Credentials ▼]
Credential Details

Attribute	Value
UserName	oracle
Password	******

More Details

***Figure 2-9.** Configuring the provisioning profile for the WebLogic domain to be used with the software library setup*

Ensure the credentials are set properly, creating new ones if necessary, but hopefully by this time you will have created preferred credentials, as is best practice.

Once you have verified that the information on the Configure page of the wizard is correct, click Next.

If you are satisfied with the information on the Review page (no upload of any files is required, so don't be alarmed when it shows that there aren't any files at this time in the bottom section), click Save and Upload.

A job will now be submitted for the task, and you will receive confirmation (Figure 2-10).

📄**Confirmation**
The entity 'WL_Profile_EM1' has been created successfully in 'Profile_Home' folder. A job 'FMW Profile_0.19410116925214704' has been submitted for uploading the files.

***Figure 2-10.** Confirmation of job submittal for the WebLogic Domain Provisioning Profile creation*

As the job is managed by the Enterprise Manager Job Service, you can now click on Enterprise, Jobs, and Job Activity to monitor the job like any other job submitted through this feature (Figure 2-11).

Job Activity

Status [Active ▼] Name [ ] [Go] Advanced Search
☑ **TIP** By default, results for the last 24 hours are displayed. Use 'Advanced Search' for more options.

View Results | Edit | Create Like | Copy To Library | Suspend | Resume | Stop | Delete | View [Runs ▼] Create Job [OS Command ▼] [Go]

Select	Name	Status (Executions)	Scheduled ▽	Targets	Target Type	Owner	Job Type
⦿	FMW PROFILE_0.19410116925214704	1 Running	Jan 5, 2014 7:56:48 PM GMT-06:00	dfwrepdb1.containerstore.com	Host	SYSMAN	createFMWBundle

***Figure 2-11.** Monitoring the provisioning profile job within the Job Activity view in the EM12c console*

You may need to refresh the console view as the job is running and then again after the job has completed. You may need to change the Activity view status to All or Successful in order to view the completed job. The job takes a significant amount of time, but you can see the job directory on the server within the working directory in which you choose to place the working files (for this example, I chose to create a temp folder in /u01/home/oracle/, as shown in Figure 2-12).

```
oracle@                     .com       :/u01/home/oracle/temp>ls
Job_EF44CB2A12716F9BE043200B14AC7D53
```

Figure 2-12. Viewing the job status from the command line via the working files that were created as part of the job

Once the job has completed you can verify that it has done so successfully in one of three ways:

- Check the Job Activity Details to ensure all steps were completed successfully.

- Click on Enterprise, Patching and Provisioning, then on Middleware and check that the profile you just created is listed.

- Click on Enterprise, Patching and Provisioning, then on Software Library. If you expand the Networks folder into its sub-directories, you will be able to see each of the three components that made up the profile, and they all should show a successful status.

Filtering Out Fusion Middleware

With the provisioning profile out of the way, you can now reduce the number of procedures in your onscreen list by filtering out Fusion Middleware. This is done by creating a new properties file template for a Fusion Middleware Provisioning Procedure (FMWPROV) procedure by the corresponding Global Universal Identifier (GUID). The FMWPROV procedure is submitted to completion using the updated properties file.

To capture the GUID for the deployment procedure, the emcli command is as follows:

```
> emcli get_procedures | grep FMWPROV
```

Your result will be the following:

```
<proc_guid>, <procedure_type>, <display_name>, <version>, <parent_name>
```

Output appears like:

```
> emcli get_procedures | grep FMWPROV
F5143FC2A0D94E37E043BB76F00ADE34 FMW Provisioning FMWPROV_DP Provision Middleware 5.0 ORACLE
```

Using the GUID above, prepare the properties file template:

```
> emcli describe_procedure_input -procedure=F5143FC2A0D94E37E043BB76F00ADE34 >FMVtmp.properties
> A properties file with the name FMVtmp.properties is created
```

Once the file is created, open the file with vi and update it with those properties required to complete the necessary data for the FMV provisioning (seen in red in Figure 2-13; will need to be updated with the values for your environment):

```
STAGING_HOST.*.name=HOST1.us.oracle.com
STAGING_HOST.*.type=LINUX_X64
STAGING_HOST.*.normalHostCreds=NC_43893_HOST1
STAGING_HOST.*.WORK_LOC=/u01/staging/prod_lib/files
DEST_FMW_HOST.*.name=FMW_HOST2
DEST_FMW_HOST.*.type=LINUX_X64
DEST_FMW_HOST.*.normalHostCreds=NC_89343_FMWHOST2
DEST_FMW_HOST.*.FMW_HOME_DEST_FMW_HOST=/u01/app/middleware/
DEST_FMW_HOST.*.WLS_HOME_DEST_FMW_HOST=FMW_HOST2
DEST_FMW_HOST.*.ORACLE_HOME_DEST_FMW_HOST=/u01/app/oracle/product/dbhome_1
DEST_FMW_HOST.*.WORK_DIR_LOC_DEST_FMW_HOST=/u01/staging/prod_lib/files
DEST_FMW_HOST.*.JRE_LOC=/usr/bin/jre/1.6/bin
DEST_FMW_HOST.*.OUI_HOME=/u01/app/orainventory
```

Figure 2-13. *Example of filled-out properties file to be used in fulfilling request for procedure calls with EM CLI*

Save the updated template file and submit the procedure to complete the provisioning:

```
> emcli submit_procedure -input_file=data:FMVtmp.properties -procedure=
F5143FC2A0D94E37E043BB76F00ADE34
```

One of the biggest strengths of provisioning is scalability. EM12c offers the opportunity to increase the cluster's capacity with additional server instances. The option to scale a managed server up and out–using EM CLI commands along with the SCALEUP procedure and the instance GUID–is required in order to create the input properties file for the procedure. Once the properties file is updated, the SCALEUP procedure can be submitted:

```
> emcli get_procedures | grep SCALEUP
B95E01B1F145B5EEE050634DC8854DC, FMW Provisioning, SCALEUP DP, Scale up/Scale out Middleware, 2.0,
ORACLE
```

Once this information is returned, you can use the GUID information to create the properties file. This process must be submitted at least once for the target GUID to create the properties file or an error will occur:

```
> emcli get_instance_data -instance= B95E01B1F145B5EEE050634DC8854DC > instancetmp.properties
A properties file with the name instancetmp.properties is created.
```

Open the properties file in an editor and enter the updated information, then save. Once updates are completed, you must submit the procedure:

```
> emcli submit_procedure -input_file: instancetmp.properties
-procedure=B95E01B1F145B5EEE050634DC8854DC
```

This will complete the process of submitting the procedure to scale up a middleware deployment.

Jython

Python has been around for quite a while and will continue to grow in popularity as a relatively easy and robust development language. But what is "Jython"?

Jython, by the simplest definition, is the Java implementation of the Python language. Like Python, the syntax is simple to learn, self-formatted, and does not require compilation (like Perl) before the code can be used.

Beginning with EM12c Release 3, the EM CLI includes an embedded Jython interpreter. The function calls, also known as verbs, are executed with their corresponding key-value pairs or parameters presented as verb arguments. The purpose and use of verbs is explained later in this book.

If utilizing interactive mode, the interpreter opens a shell where simpler commands are issued, rather than shell-scripting mode where the interpreter accepts a scripted list of commands to process as a program, or rather than when simply exercising EM CLI at the command prompt. The advantage, of course, is that end-users can apply the power of EM CLI without being concerned about syntax and key-value pairs.

You can connect to any target in the Enterprise Manager environment via stateless communication and a security layer in the OMS so as to utilize Jython with EM CLI. There is a simple and generic list function within the Enterprise Manager resources, as well as an ability to run user-defined SQL queries to access published repository views.

To execute a script written in Jython, the command can be as simple as executing it from the command line interactively, much as you would a SQL script:

```
> emcli @test_python_scrpt.py
```

To run in interactive mode, you would need to start the EM CLI program:

```
> emcli <enter>
emcli>
```

The Jython-based scripting environment allows interactive processing and a simple scripting mode with a standardized format using JSON. JSON stands for Java.Script Object Notation. JSON format is also fairly simple. It requires only the representative data for collections of names and value pairs. These pairs are then housed within arrays, maps, or lists to ensure manageability.

Similar to XML, JSON corresponds to how both developers and environment systems read data, but it doesn't have the metadata overhead that is required for XML, referred to as elements and attribute names.

Supported Java Versions

EM CLI requires proper Java version support, which is also a requirement for advanced scripting with Jython, so knowledge of Java versions is important. The copy of EM CLI installed on your OMS during standard product installation relies on the JAVA_HOME already in place for OEM.

EM CLI on other locations (such as your desktop) must have the JAVA_HOME set, and it requires Java version 1.6.0.43 or greater.

If using Jython, Java must be installed and set before installing the EM CLI advanced kit (emcliadvancedkit.jar). Windows 8 and 8.1 will experience errors unless Java version 1.7.0.17 is present. Compatibility matrices are available at My Oracle Support.

■ **Tip** Windows servers will often recommend uninstalling older versions of Java once new ones are in place. To avoid registry issues, ensure that:

- no other ORACLE_HOME is utilizing the Java version in its path, and

- the older version of Java is uninstalled *before* installing the newer version to prevent any impact to the new installation.

Path and Environment Variables

To execute EM CLI verbs, no matter if they are Python or otherwise, you will need a connection to the OMS. This will require environment variables to be set (also known as client properties) as part of the EM CLI scripting environment. You can inspect all possible client properties by utilizing the help option in the EM CLI:

```
> emcli>help('client_properties')
        EMCLI_OMS_URL
        EMCLI_USERNAME
        EMCLI_AUTOLOGIN
        EMCLI_TRUSTALL
        EMCLI_VERBJAR_DIR
        EMCLI_CERT_LOC
        EMCLI_LOG_LOC
        EMCLI_LOG_LEVEL
        EMCLI_OUTPUT_TYPE(status())
```

Client or Remote Target Installation

There are various reasons for installing the EM CLI on a remote target. You must decide if there is a significant need to do so or if a task that needs to be run from the remote target can be accomplished with an emctl command instead. Here are two reasons for not installing the EM CLI on a remote target or client:

1. Security: The EM CLI will be configured to access the OMS, and the security risk of doing so should be justified. Any person using the EM CLI on the remote target or client will still be required to log in as they would from the OMS installation of the EM CLI, but this does pose an added security risk versus a solely OMS-installed configuration.

2. Efficiency: Enterprise Manager Control (EMCTL) command can accomplish several of the same tasks as EM CLI at the command line, such as issuing a remote blackout of a target and so forth. In those cases, there is no need to go through a full remote installation and configuration of EM CLI. EMCTL uses the existing EM agent to perform those tasks, using its standard connections without the need for additional passwords or authentication tokens.

Now we will review the steps to follow when you have a justified reason to proceed with a remote target or client installation of the EM CLI. Desktop installation of the EM CLI client is also accomplished with this procedure.

Downloading and deploying the EM CLI client to remote hosts requires only a few steps. The actual EM CLI installation was completed automatically on the OMS host, so only remote client installations are required to be done manually. There are two kits that come as part of the EM CLI client–the EM CLI standard kit and the EM CLI scripting kit. If you wish to use the scripting method outside of the OMS host, then both kits are required for the remote installation. The scripting kit includes the Jython interpreter, so a secondary interpreter is not required for Jython scripting.

This section will focus solely on the standard kit, while the next section will enhance the installation technique by focusing on the advanced (both standard and scripting) kit.

Before installing, you must meet the following requirements on any client or remote target:

- EM12c Cloud Control Framework

- Java Version 1.6x or higher

- Operating System Linux, Sun, HPUX, AIX, or Windows.

Once these requirements have been met, you must download the kit(s) from one of two places. The first it through the EM12c console by clicking on Setup, Command Line Interface, then choosing "Download the EM CLI Standard Kit to your Workstation." Choose a location to which to save the download.

You can also download it from the OMS Host using the URL link:

```
https://<OMS_HOST>:<port>/em/<swlib_directory>/emcli/kit/emclikit.jar
```

Once you have completed the download of the emclikit.jar file, copy it via SCP/FTP or other transport utility to the remote server.

Upon completing the transfer of the .jar file, as with any kit installation, ensure your JAVA_HOME is set. Depending on your operating system, this may require one of the following:

Unix:

```
> setenv JAVA_HOME /usr/local/packages/j2sdk
> setenv PATH $JAVA_HOME/bin:$PATH
> echo $JAVA_HOME
> echo $PATH
```

Linux:

```
> export JAVA_HOME /usr/bin/jdk6/jre
> export PATH $JAVA_HOME/bin:$PATH
> echo $JAVA_HOME $PATH
```

Windows:

```
> set JAVA_HOME D:\progra~1\java\jre
> echo %JAVA_HOME%
```

■ **Note** The path will be set in the server's environment variable.

Then check the Java path as follows:
Unix/Linux:

```
> which java
```

Windows:

```
C:\users: where java
```

Once the JAVA_HOME is verified, the EM CLI standard kit can be quickly installed by executing the following command, replacing the emcli_install_dir with the associated directory in which you wish to install the EM CLI:

```
> $JAVA_HOME/bin/java -jar emclikit.jar -install_dir=<em_cli_home_dir>
```

For Windows, the process is adjusted to take changes for environment variables into consideration:

```
%JAVA_HOME%\bin\java -jar emclikit.jar -install_dir=<em_cli_home_dir>
```

Once complete, the following message will be returned:

```
The EM CLI client is installed in <emcli_client_install_dir>
```

This will verify that the installation is complete. You will need to review the logs and ensure that there were no errors in the installation; also check that all functionality is enabled. If you use Single Sign-on (SSO) or other advanced security, ensure that there are steps taken to include synchronization with the EM CLI.

EM CLI Advanced Kit

As with the standard kit, the EM CLI advanced kit can be downloaded from the EM12c console. Once logged in to the Enterprise Environment, click on Setup, then on Command Line Interface (Figure 2-14).

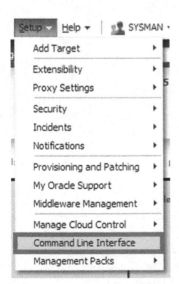

Figure 2-14. *Accessing the EM CLI from the Enterprise Manager console*

Once you've entered the EM CLI installation wizard, you will see the choices shown in Figure 2-15.

EMCLI with Scripting option

EMCLI with Scripting option is a comprehensive kit that includes EMCLI Standard features as well. It has an embedded Jython scripting engine to build Jython scripts for automating tasks on Enterprise Manager.

Download and Deploy steps

- Download the EMCLI with Scripting option kit to your workstation.

- Set your JAVA_HOME environment variable and ensure that it is part of your PATH. You must be running Java 1.6.0_43 or greater. For example:
    - setenv JAVA_HOME /usr/local/packages/j2sdk
    - setenv PATH $JAVA_HOME/bin:$PATH

- You can install EMCLI with Scripting option in any directory either on the same machine as the OMS or on any machine on your network (download the emcliadvancedkit.jar to that machine).
    - java -jar emcliadvancedkit.jar client -install_dir=<emcli client dir>

- Execute "emcli help sync" from the EMCLI Home (the directory where you have installed emcli) for instructions on how to use the "sync" verb to configure the client for a particular OMS.

- By default EMCLI with Scripting option doesn't store any user session information on disk. It is tailored to build production grade Jython modules for EM. To use features of EMCLI standard you can to re-setup it using the information provided above for EMCLI Standard.

- Refer to readme.txt file in client install directory for more information on interactive shell and scripting support.

Figure 2-15. *Installation requirements for the EM CLI installation from the Enterprise Manager console*

The instructions on the right-hand side of the page give clear and defined steps on how to download the kit and which pre-requisites are required to complete the installation successfully.

EMCLI Installation via the OMS

The last option for installation is performed through the OMS. You will initially download the EM CLI kit to the remote host or your workstation. Note that the download link is the first bulleted option in the display page, "Download the EM CLI with scripting options to your workstation."

Click on this link to start the download process. As this is a Java file, you may receive the following or similar warning (Figure 2-16):

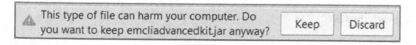

Figure 2-16. *Warning when downloading the .jar file required for a workstation download of the EM CLI installation*

You can also download the file directly via this URL:

`http://<EM_HOST>:<port>/em/<public_sw_lib>/emcli/kit/emcliadvancedkit.jar`

Once this is complete, ensure you've copied the file to the new host via SCP/FTP or another file transfer utility. If the advanced kit is to be used on the local OMS host, then proceed with the installation step.

Ensure that you've set your JAVA_HOME properly and that it's part of your environment path, which we covered in the standard kit installation steps.

■ **Note** If this is for a Windows host installation, set the JAVA_HOME in the environment variables and not at the session level. Oracle installs invariably call secondary sessions that may not carry over the session-level variables, which can cause a failure in those secondary processes.

Execute the installation step with the following command, replacing emcli_install_dir with the directory associated with the installation path:

```
> java -jar emcliadvancedkit.jar client -install_dir=<emcli_install_dir>
```

As before, the following message will return upon successful installation:

```
The EM CLI client is installed in <emcli_install_dir>
```

Post-Installation

Once the installation is complete for any kit, on host or remote host, synchronization with the OMS should be performed.

You first need to configure the EM CLI client or remote host information with the existing OMS before synchronizing with it.

Change over to the EM CLI home directory and set up a local user with local configuration information. You can easily collect information on the setup verb by typing in the following command:

```
> emcli help setup
```

Setting up a local user requires the following command syntax:
Standard Kit:

```
> emcli setup -url=http://<local_host_name>:<port>/em -username=em_user
```

Advanced (Scripting) Kit

```
> emcli setup -url=http://<local_host_name>:<port>/em -username=em_user -trustall
> emcli login -username=sysman
```

Once set up, you need to synchronize it with the OMS:

```
> emcli help sync
```

Patching and Upgrades

Although patching and upgrades may not first appear to be part of installation, they are a very important aspect of it. Considering that we stress the importance of applying any and all bundle patches upon installation, the inclusion of checking for these during the installation process should relay how important this step is in the installation of any OEM environment.

Patching with the EM CLI Clients

Patching can be performed by utilizing deployment procedures from the command-line interface as completely as it can be performed via the Enterprise Manager console. Patching is performed in conjunction with a properties file, which includes the inputs to ease commands and offers the information the EM CLI requires to complete the patching process. It's important to remember that EM CLI is not an agent like the regular EM agent on each host; it is a utility that installs as client software.

To create a properties file from scratch, you need to know how and when to create one, using one of the following steps:

- from a template from an existing procedure

- using a properties file in its current state, created via the console

- re-using a saved properties file from a previous execution

Creating a Properties File from a Template

Using an existing procedure GUID, a template can be built with just a few commands and values inserted for the new procedure that you want to execute.

Then perform the execution of the EM CLI command to pull info about the procedure templates available. For our example below, we are going to pull patching template examples:

```
./emcli get_procedures -type=PatchOracleSoftware
CF9D698E8D3843B9E043200B14ACB8B3, PatchOracleSoftware, CLONE_PATCH_SIDB, Clone and Patch Oracle
Database, 12.2, ORACLE
CF9D698E8D4743B9E043200B14ACB8B3, PatchOracleSoftware, PATCH_ALL_NODES_CLUSTER_ASM, Patch Oracle
Cluster ASM - All Nodes, 12.2, ORACLE
```

The first information returned is the procedure GUID that we require to then create our properties file from which to work:

```
./emcli describe_procedure_input -procedure=CF9D698E8D3843B9E043200B14ACB8B3
> Patch_template.properties
Verifying parameters ...
```

And your template file is now created:

```
-rw-r--r-- 1 oracle dba    65950 Jan 27 19:12 Patch_template.properties
```

Patching Remote Client Installations

If you have EM CLI clients deployed to target servers, it is simple to track them by registering them with the OMS as part of the EM CLI setup. Tracking information is retained in the OMS on all EM CLI client installation binaries that require patching. It will also identify EM CLI installations that need to be updated with new passwords or synced with new verbs from the OMS repository. Client software installations are not targets in OEM, so they are not tracked or monitored by the EM agents.

EM Security Framework

Security is always on the top of anyone's mind given the power behind the EM CLI. The command line has access to the entire monitored environment, so it's no surprise that this topic is included here.

As is standard with any Oracle security practice, hardening of servers–removing services and access to direct OS-level files that are part of Oracle–is recommended as part of a security exercise.

Basic security design requires that we look from all monitored targets up through the Enterprise Manager components, but there are white papers to address concerns outside of the EM CLI; we will focus on the command line and Enterprise Manager in this section.

Security in the EM CLI

The security architecture for the EM CLI is built around the architecture in the Enterprise Manager 12c environment and is often the first point of security concerns, as we've discussed above. The single point of access to the Enterprise Manager via the EM CLI is the second concern. The credentials to the remote targets that you will be interacting with via the EM CLI are the third level of access and are of even more concern, as these targets most likely include the production targets of your database environment.

Secure Mode for EM CLI Setup

Looking at the second level of security, we will discuss what secure mode means in the EM CLI. Secure mode EM CLI, which is the installation mode by default, does not store any Enterprise Manager or SSO passwords on local disk or in logs and files.

By default, the EM CLI login automatically times out after reaching a set point for inactivity, and the user must log in again before attempting to issue any other commands via the EM CLI.

If you wish to set up the EM CLI installation to log in automatically upon re-issue of a verb and demand an explicit logout of the EM CLI, execute the following command:

```
> emcli setup -noautologin
```

HTTPS Trusted Certificate

Setting up HTTPS trusted certificates first requires a quick check to verify it hasn't already been done. This can be achieved with an EM CLI status after the following sync, as shown in Figure 2-17:

```
> emcli status
```

```
        emcli status
Oracle Enterprise Manager 12c Release 4 EM CLI.
Copyright (c) 1996, 2014 Oracle Corporation and/or its affiliates. All rights reserved.

Instance Home          : /u01/app/gc_inst/em/EMGC_OMS1/sysman/emcli/setup/.emcli
Verb Jars Home         : /u01/app/middleware/oms/bin/./bindings/12.1.0.4.0/.emcli
Status                 : Configured
EM CLI Home            : /u01/app/middleware/oms/bin/.
EM CLI Version         : 12.1.0.4.0
Java Home              : /u01/app/middleware/jdk16/jdk/jre
Java Version           : 1.6.0_43
Log file               : /u01/app/gc_inst/em/EMGC_OMS1/sysman/emcli/setup/.emcli/.emcli.log
EM URL                 : https://        :.us.oracle.com:7802/em
EM user                : sys:
Auto login             : false
Trust all_certificates : true
```

Figure 2-17. Issuing the status call from the EM CLI to view information about the Enterprise Manager Command-Line Interface and https status

Check the EM URL value to see if a secure HTTPS URL is already being used for the connection. If not, this can be configured with an EM CLI verb call:

```
> emcli setup -url="http[s]://host:port/em" -username="<username>" [-trustall] [-novalidate]
```

You will be asked to provide the SYSMAN password to complete this security-level configuration change to the EM console. Enter the password and press Return to complete the setup. Running the emcli status verb call will show the updated value for the EMURL, or one can use the emcli setup call to view it (Figure 2-18).

```
            emcli setup
Oracle Enterprise Manager 12c Release 4.
Copyright (c) 1996, 2014 Oracle Corporation and/or its affiliates. All rights reserved.

Instance Home          : /u01/app/gc_inst/em/EMGC_OMS1/sysman/emcli/setup/.emcli
Verb Jars Home         : /u01/app/middleware/oms/bin/./bindings/12.1.0.4.0/.emcli
EM URL                 : https://        .us.oracle.com:7802/em
EM user                : sysman
Trust all certificates : true
Auto login             : false
```

Figure 2-18. *Issuing the* setup *command to verify a secure https connection for the EM URL used by the EM CLI and Enterprise Manager console*

Verbs of Great Value in Release 4

As with each of the EM12c releases, there have been great enhancements and the introduction of new verbs to be used with the EM CLI. Release 4 (12.1.0.4) was no different, and there were updated patches to complete the release, as dependencies for the verbs from other product lines were released as well.

Gold Agent Update Verbs

The "gold agent" verbs were one of those verb groups that were released in a patch versus being part of the initial Release 4. They were listed with the initial EM CLI release documentation and help file, but were not actually available until the patch. See here:

> get_agent_update_status: Shows all agent update results using a gold image

> get_not_updatable_agents: Shows agents that can't be updated as part of a gold image

> get_updatable_agents: Shows updatable agents for a given gold agent image name or part of a gold image series

BI Publisher Reports Verbs

Release 4 included BI Publisher as part of the installation. The compact install, which is now only approximately 300 MB in size, required only a few EM CLI commands to grant access and features to an Enterprise Manager user:

> grant_bipublisher_roles: Grants access to the BI Publisher catalog and features

> revoke_bipublisher_roles: Revokes access to the BI Publisher catalog and features

Cloud Service Verbs

Cloud offerings improved significantly with Release 4, and the ability to manage cloud requests, users, and service-instance data from the command line was essential to simplifying task management for cloud services:

cancel_cloud_service_requests: Cancel the cloud requests. Either user or names option should be provided

delete_cloud_service_instances: Deletes the cloud service instances based on the specified filter

delete_cloud_user_objects: Deletes cloud user objects, including cloud service instances and requests

get_cloud_service_instances: Retrieves the list of cloud service instances. All instances will be printed if no option is specified.

get_cloud_service_requests: Retrieves the list of cloud requests. All requests will be printed if no filter is applied.

get_cloud_user_objects: Retrieves the list of cloud user objects, including cloud service instances and requests. All objects will be printed if user option is not used.

Miscellaneous Verbs

There were significant changes to blackouts in Release 4, one of which was to allow for retroactive blackouts within the console, as well as within the command line:

create_rbk: Creates retroactive blackout on given targets and updates their availability. The retroactive blackout feature needs to be enabled from the UI for using this emcli command.

Orphan targets have been an issue for a while. Having the new compliance-enhancement verb addresses this problem:

fix_compliance_state: Fix compliance state by removing references in deleted targets.

The following verb is to support the complex composite targets in WebLogic environments. Having a specific verb designed to modify these targets is essential:

modify_monitoring_agent: This verb can be used to change the agents that are configured to monitor targets in a WebLogic domain.

Fusion Middleware Provisioning Verbs

Fusion Middleware has a number of verb additions and enhancements to help manage WebLogic features and build out more options from the command line:

create_fmw_domain_profile: Creates a Fusion Middleware Provisioning Profile from a WebLogic domain

create_fmw_home_profile: Creates a Fusion Middleware Provisioning Profile from an Oracle home

create_inst_media_profile: Creates a Fusion Middleware Provisioning Profile from installation media

Job Verbs

There were a number of enhancements to the EM Job Service. These enhancements enable us to export and import jobs from one EM12c Release 2 OMS to a same version or higher environment. For better job management options, Oracle has also added more-advanced job control from the EM CLI with Release 4:

export_jobs: Exports all matching job definitions in EM, including corrective actions. System jobs and nested jobs are excluded.

import_jobs: Imports all job definitions in to EM, including corrective actions from zip files. Library jobs are created. EM CLI logged-in user is set as the library job owner.

job_input_file: Specifies some or all properties for the job verb in a property file. Properties set on the command line override values set in the file.

resume_job: Resumes a job or a set of jobs matching the filter criteria.

suspend_job: Suspends a job or a set of jobs matching the filter criteria.

Target Data Verbs

create_assoc: Creates target association instances

delete_assoc: Deletes target association instances

list_allowed_pairs: Lists allowed association types for the specified source and destination target types

list_assoc: Lists associations between the specified source and destination targets

manage_agent_partnership: Overrides Enterprise Manager's default behavior of automatically assigning partner agents to other agents. A partner agent is an agent that, in addition to its other functions, is assigned to another agent as its "partner" in order to remotely monitor the availability of that agent and its host. This verb is not meant to be commonly used. It is provided to support special circumstances where an administrator might want to explicitly assign agent partnerships or exclude agents from being partners, or exclude agents from being remotely monitored by other agents.

Summary

For most readers, verb procedural calls have been the largest consumer of EM CLI work. Being familiar with the significant verb changes in 12.1.0.4 is crucial, but for the remainder of the book, we are going to build out your knowledge with the goal of scripting within the Enterprise Manager Command-Line Interface.

CHAPTER 3

■ ■ ■

Terminology and Basics

EM CLI can seem overwhelming at first, as with any command-line utility. But like anything else in technology, the more one understands how something works, the more useful and the easier it will be to work with.

There is too much information in EM CLI to memorize even a small part of it. Documention is as critical as the tool itself. Understanding the terminology that the documentation, built-in manuals, and the tool itself use will allow you to quickly find what you need by asking the right questions. For example, if you are looking for the command to create a user, you need to know you are searching for a verb, not a parameter or a variable.

Once one understands EM CLI's terminology, a basic understanding of its functionality allows one to immediately get started with basic tasks, and that is where the real learning begins. This chapter introduces the basics of EM CLI first by explaining how it works with Enterprise Manager and then by providing a number of detailed examples.

Terminology: Verbs

EM CLI functionality uses *verbs* to perform actions. A verb is a task or action in the form of a user command that exposes Enterprise Manager functionality. Understanding verbs and how they are used to accomplish tasks is essential to fully utilizing EM CLI.

Verbs can include one or more parameters. The mode being used determines what those parameters look like. For example, when using EM CLI in command-line mode, the parameters are positional arguments that follow the verb. Each argument is preceded by a dash and followed by an equal sign. The argument may then be assigned a value, which is usually enclosed with quotation marks.

Some of the parameters are required and some are optional. The documentation identifies optional arguments by enclosing them in brackets. For example, the clear_privilege_delegation_setting verb has one required argument and two optional arguments (Listing 3-1).

Listing 3-1. Required and optional parameters for the clear_privilege_delegation_setting verb

```
emcli clear_privilege_delegation_setting
        -host_names="name1;name2;..."
        [-input_file="FILE:file_path"]
        [-force="yes/no"]
```

As of version 12.1.0.3, there are 362 verbs. To more easily help you find and manage verbs, they are grouped into 58 categories. The categories represent logical functionality. For example, if you were looking for verbs related to patching, you would find them in the *Patch Verbs* category. If you were looking for verbs related to blackouts, you would look in the *Blackout Verbs* category.

The verbs are named in a way that leaves little doubt as to what they do. Some of the names are short, such as login and start_agent, and some very long, such as update_monitoring_creds_from_agent and list_target_privilege_delegation_settings. This nomenclature has the benefit of making it relatively easy to remember verbs as well as making it easy to look up a verb based on its functionality.

Modes

EM CLI is invoked in one of three different modes. The mode is the method of using EM CLI. The decision to use one mode over another depends on the purpose and scope of the task.

Command-line

Prior to version 12.1.0.3, EM CLI operated in just one mode—command-line. In command-line mode, EM CLI executes one verb per invocation of the emcli executable. There is no subshell or programming interface for EM CLI in command-line mode. Any scripting of EM CLI needs to be done with a shell that can call individual EM CLI commands and process the output.

Interactive

With the release of version 12.1.0.3, EM CLI now includes the classic command-line mode as well as interactive and scripting modes. Interactive mode allows EM CLI to be invoked as a subshell of whatever terminal is being used. When EM CLI is running in interactive mode, the prompt changes to a custom Python prompt:

```
cd $OMS_HOME/bin
./emcli
emcli>
```

Scripting

Scripting mode does not have a subshell or a prompt. In fact, it is very similar to command-line mode, except that its invocation allows as its first parameter a script written in the Python-compatible programming language. This script is then executed as if the commands were typed into interactive mode. EM CLI in scripting mode is invoked one time but unlike while in command-line mode, the full functionality of the Python programming language can be used to do everything for which a shell is required in command-line mode. In addition, scripting mode invokes EM CLI in its native form, which makes things like parsing the output of commands much easier and more efficient, especially with the use of JSON.

Help!

EM CLI has built-in help functionality. Getting a general list of available verbs for command-line mode is as simple as executing EM CLI with the verb help. Be prepared for a large amount of data if you are not qualifying the command with additional parameters. If you need additional information on a particular verb, add the verb as the second parameter.

To use help in interactive mode, the help functionality is called by using a Python function called help(). The help() function requires only one parameter—the help topic. The help topic can be a verb function as well as certain verb function parameters. Be aware that there are help topics included in interactive mode that don't exist in command-line mode. For example, the command-line mode uses setup files to hold EM CLI properties, but interactive and scripting modes do not. The properties are set each time interactive or scripting modes are invoked. We can use the help() function to view which parameters to use to set properties, as shown in Listing 3-2.

Listing 3-2. Client properties help page

```
emcli>help('client_properties')
EMCLI_OMS_URL          : OMS URL To connect to.
EMCLI_USERNAME         : OMS Username.
EMCLI_AUTOLOGIN        : Possible values are true,false. Default is false.
EMCLI_TRUSTALL         : Possible values are true,false. Default is false.
EMCLI_VERBJAR_DIR      : Location of bindings directory.
EMCLI_CERT_LOC         : Location of a valid certificate file.
EMCLI_LOG_LOC          : Directory where log files will be stored.
EMCLI_LOG_LEVEL        : Possible values are ALL,INFO,FINE,FINER,WARN,SEVERE. Default is SEVERE.
EMCLI_OUTPUT_TYPE      : Possible values are json, JSON, text, TEXT. Default is json in script
                         mode and text in interactive mode.
```

status() will list values of all the client properties. set_client_property(propertyname,value) and get_client_property(propertyname) can be used to set and get a client property.

Understanding Error Codes

There are a number of error codes that you might see when using EM CLI. The information provided in these error codes is critical to determining what caused the error. The error codes shown below are some of those that are seen most often; they almost always have an easy fix.

Command-line mode requires a login session to be established before any commands can be executed. In secure environments and by default, the login session will expire after 45 minutes. When a valid command is executed without an established login session when in command-line mode, an error is thrown with an exit code of 255. In order to proceed, a valid session will need to be established by using the login verb, as shown in listing 3-3.

Listing 3-3. Login error message and exit code in command-line mode

```
[oracle oms]$ emcli get_targets
Error: Session expired. Run emcli login to establish a session.
[oracle oms]$ echo $?
255
```

Interactive and scripting modes require that the connection parameters be included each time a script is executed or an interactive session is established. If the connection URL has not been specified, an error will be thrown with details on how to establish the connection, as shown in listing 3-4.

Listing 3-4. Settings error in interactive and scripting modes

```
emcli>get_targets()
Error: EM URL is not set. Do set_client_property('EMCLI_OMS_URL', '<value>')
Or set it as environment variable.

[oracle ~]$ emcli @test.py
Traceback (most recent call last):
  File "test.py", line 1, in <module>
    get_targets()
```

```
File "<string>", line 41, in get_targets
emcli.exception.VerbExecutionError: Error: EM URL is not set.
Do set_client_property('EMCLI_OMS_URL', '<value>')
Or set it as environment variable.
```

Errors can be caused by myriad reasons. The EM CLI developers have done an excellent job of making the error messages descriptive and useful. When you encounter errors, read the description thoroughly in order to understand what issue caused it. When in doubt, search for the error in the documentation or on the Internet. Chances are, someone else has already found and fixed the cause of the error.

Syntax

The EM CLI program can be used in three different modes. These are command-line mode, interactive mode, and scripting mode. Up until version 12.1.0.2, there was only the command-line mode. The interactive and scripting modes became available in version 12.1.0.3, along with an exposed programming interface that uses Jython.

The standard command-line mode hasn't changed much since Grid Control 10g. With few exceptions, scripts used with previous versions of EM CLI will continue to work with the latest version or 12c. The command-line syntax is the emcli command, followed by one verb, followed by zero or more verb options or parameters, as shown in this example:

```
emcli create_group -name=my_group -add_targets="mymachine.example.com:hostname"
```

The interactive and scripting modes both use the Jython programming language. The interactive mode is a single-user interactive session created by executing the emcli command without any parameters.

Standard Linux shell commands will not work in the interactive shell. The interactive mode of EM CLI can be closed using the command exit() or by typing ctrl-d in Linux or ctrl-z in Windows.

Interactive mode syntax differs from that of the standard command-line mode. Once an interactive mode shell has been established, it is no longer necessary to use the emcli command. Executing an EM CLI command is done by putting a verb into the shell directly and enclosing the verb options within parentheses. The verb options are not preceded by a dash like they are in command-line mode, but rather are preceded by a comma when followed by other options. The following shows the create_group function in interactive mode with the name and add_targets options:

```
emcli> create_group(name=my_group, add_targets="mymachine.example.com:hostname")
```

Scripting mode uses the same command syntax as the interactive mode but does not require the Jython shell. All of the EM CLI commands to be executed would be formatted like the interactive shell command above and put into a script, along with any other Python code to be included. The script is executed non-interactively by following the emcli command with an @ symbol and the name of the script:

```
[oracle ~]$ emcli @my_script.py
```

Setup

EM CLI is included in every OMS installation and is set up to connect to that OMS automatically. The setup configuration can be confirmed with the setup verb. Running the command in command-line mode shows that EM CLI is configured to connect to https://oem.example.com:7802/em with the SYSMAN user, as shown in Listing 3-5.

Listing 3-5. Output of EM CLI setup in command-line mode

```
[oracle ~]$ emcli status
Oracle Enterprise Manager 12c EMCLI12.1.0.3.0.
Copyright (c) 1996, 2013 Oracle Corporation and/or its affiliates. All rights reserved.

Instance Home            : /u01/app/oracle/product/12.1.0/gc_inst/em/EMGC_OMS1/sysman/
                           emcli/setup/.emcli
Verb Jars Home           : null
Status                   : Configured
EMCLI Home               : /u01/app/oracle/product/12.1.0/mw_1/oms/bin
EMCLI Version            : 12.1.0.3.0
Java Home                : /u01/app/oracle/product/12.1.0/mw_1/jdk16/jdk/jre
Java Version             : 1.6.0_43
Log file                 : /u01/app/oracle/product/12.1.0/gc_inst/em/EMGC_OMS1/sysman/
                           emcli/setup/.emcli/.emcli.log
EM URL                   : https://oem.example.com:7802/em
EM user                  : SYSMAN
Auto login               : false
Trust all certificates   : true
```

After installing EM CLI on a system other than the OMS server, it must be explicitly configured before it will function with an Enterprise Manager installation. Executing the setup command against an EM CLI installation that has not yet been configured returns an error, as shown in Listing 3-6.

Listing 3-6. An EM CLI installation that has not yet been set up

```
[oracle ~]$ emcli setup
Oracle Enterprise Manager 12c 3.
Copyright (c) 1996, 2013 Oracle Corporation and/or its affiliates. All rights reserved.

No current OMS
```

The configuration is done with the setup verb followed by a number of parameters. The url parameter is the same as the address used in the browser to login to Enterprise Manager. The dir parameter specifies the directory in which to install the client. The username parameter indicates which username the client will use for connecting. This noautologin parameter determines that a user name and password will need to be provided in order to gain access to the OMS before an EM CLI session can be established. The trustall parameter indicates that certificates on the OMS will be trusted automatically. The following dir parameter in the EM CLI setup command is using shell expansion to indicate that the installation directory is the current working directory:

```
[oracle ~]$ emcli -url=https://<hostname of grid server>:1159/em -dir=$(pwd)
-username=<username> -noautologin -trustall
```

Running the setup command in interactive mode reveals that neither the URL nor the user has been defined. This is because these parameters must be set each time for both interactive and scripting modes, as shown in Listing 3-7.

Listing 3-7. Executing the setup function in interactive mode

```
emcli>status()
Oracle Enterprise Manager 12c EMCLI with Scripting option Version 12.1.0.3.0.
Copyright (c) 1996, 2013 Oracle Corporation and/or its affiliates. All rights reserved.

Verb Jars Home (EMCLI_VERBJAR_DIR)    : /u01/app/oracle/product/12.1.0/mw_1/oms/bin/bindings/
                                        default/.emcli
EMCLI Home (EMCLI_INSTALL_HOME)       : /u01/app/oracle/product/12.1.0/mw_1/oms/bin
EMCLI Version                         : 12.1.0.3.0
Java Home                             : /u01/app/oracle/product/12.1.0/mw_1/jdk16/jdk/jre
Java Version                          : 1.6.0_43
Log file (EMCLI_LOG_LOC)              : CONSOLE
Log level (EMCLI_LOG_LEVEL)           : SEVERE
EM URL (EMCLI_OMS_URL)                : NOT SET
EM user (EMCLI_USERNAME)              : NOT SET
Auto login (EMCLI_AUTOLOGIN)          : false
Trust all certificates (EMCLI_TRUSTALL) : false
```

Once the setup is complete and a valid Enterprise Manager has been authenticated, EM CLI will be ready to carry out tasks against EM. Setup is often where problems can be found, especially during the initial setup. For example, you may not know that the port used by EM is blocked between the server on which EM CLI was installed and the OMS. The setup process will reveal this fact. Once a connection has been established with a successful login, the EM CLI setup process is complete.

Communication

A number of tasks can be accomplished with either EM CLI or EMCTL. The choice of which tool to use will depend on a number of factors, such as which tool is available to use or which is more efficient for a particular task. The method in which the tool will interface with Enterprise Manager may be an additional factor to consider.

EM CLI

EM CLI is a client of the Oracle Management Server (OMS) just as SQL*plus is a client of the database. The Enterprise Manager OMS installation includes an installation of EM CLI. The EM CLI executable is located in the OMS home directory, <OMS_HOME>/bin/emctl. EM CLI communicates with the OMS using HTML through the same port and URL that is used to access the Enterprise Manager graphical interface.

A network trace run on the port used for HTTP communication between EM CLI and Enterprise Manager would show that all of the requests from EM CLI are GET and POST requests via HTTP. These are the same requests that come from the GUI console when establishing a logon.

The way EM CLI interfaces with Enterprise Manager allows it to connect from any location where a network connection can be established to the IP and port of the OMS, which gives EM CLI a distinct advantage over EMCTL in cases where the commands need to be run from a server other than the one hosting the OMS agent.

EMCTL

EMCTL communicates directly with the agent with which it is installed. EMCTL will only communicate with its own agent, even when other agents are running on the same server.

> ■ **Note** There is also an EMCTL interface that controls and communicates directly with the OMS and it has a completely different set of commands.

The emctl command located in <AGENT_BASE>/agent_inst/bin is a shell or batch script that sets environment variables and executes the <AGENT_HOME>/bin/emctl command with the parameters fed to the first command. The <AGENT_HOME>/bin/emctl is also a shell or batch script that sets environment variables as well as sources a number of other files. It then executes a perl script with the parameters fed to the first command. This perl script sources a number of other perl scripts and either reads existing state files or interacts directly with the java agent process for a result.

Because EMCTL interacts directly with the java agent process, it is not considered a client. This also means that the agent cannot be remotely controlled using EMCTL.

EMCTL versus EM CLI

When to use EMCTL versus EM CLI is largely based on preference and environment limitations. For example, both commands can control blackouts in Enterprise Manager. In one environment, there may be a limitation on installing the EM CLI remotely or locally because of the Java version it requires or the port access it needs, making EMCTL the better option. In another environment, there may be a restriction on shell access on an agent server, making EM CLI the better option. Understanding the architecture differences between EMCTL and EM CLI will help with the decision of using one versus the other in different circumstances.

The syntax of EM CLI is relatively straightforward; emcli followed by a verb, followed by mandatory and optional parameters. The syntax of EMCTL is not as easy to understand and does not follow a strict format.

For most commands the format is as follows: emctl followed by a verb, followed by agent. For some configuration commands the format is: emctl followed by config agent, followed by a verb such as listtargets or secure. Generally, the easiest way to figure out the syntax of the EMCTL command you want to execute is to look up the documentation online or to print out the help text by executing the emctl command without any arguments. The help text will print to the screen.

This help text can be made searchable by redirecting it to a file that can be opened and searched or by piping the output to a searchable line reader such as less:

```
emctl > help.txt; vim help.txt
emctl | less
```

Now that we've reviewed a number of important concepts and definitions, let's look at some real-world examples that can be used to accomplish many of the most common tasks for which one might use EM CLI.

The first task, Login, is one that must be done for each session of EM CLI, regardless of which mode is used. The other tasks are examples of using EM CLI when the GUI is not a suitable option, such as within scheduled scripts or when working with large numbers of targets.

Task: Establish a Login

There is little useful functionality of EM CLI without having a connection to an OMS. Creating that connection is usually the first step of using the interface. How to establish a connection depends on the mode being used.

When using command-line mode, a login will not need to be established if the -autologin parameter was specified during setup, since this parameter indicates that the credentials used during the install of EM CLI are stored in the installation files and are used for every command automatically. A login is established using the login verb. The login verb must be followed by the -username parameter and can optionally be followed by the -password parameter.

It is inadvisable to include the password on the command line because of the security implications of exposed passwords. If the password is not included as a parameter, EM CLI will prompt the user for a password, and the characters entered will not be echoed to the screen, nor will the password be exposed when looking at the running processes using the ps command. If the -autologin parameter was not specified during setup, a login session will prompt for a password:

```
[oracle ~]$ emcli login -username=sysman
Enter password :

Login successful
```

In the case of running EM CLI in scripting or interactive mode, the login information must be explicitly given for each script execution and at the beginning of each interactive session. These two modes do not use the credentials established during setup, even if the -autologin parameter was used.

A simple script can be created to establish a connection and can be used in both interactive and scripting modes. The login script needs to specify the URL by which to connect, the SSL authentication method, and a login credential. Both of these modes expect a Python script (Listing 3-8).

Listing 3-8. Login script to be used in interactive and scripting modes

```
from emcli import *

set_client_property('EMCLI_OMS_URL', 'https://oem.example.com:7802/em')
set_client_property('EMCLI_TRUSTALL', 'true')

myLogin(username='sysman')

myLogin()
```

Placing this text in a file with an extension of .py makes it a module that can be imported into EM CLI. For example, the script can be called login.py and placed in the /home/oracle/scripts directory. However, EM CLI will not necessarily be able to find the script, because this path is not in the default Jython path. Explicitly defining the Jython search path will guarantee that any scripts within that search path can be imported by EM CLI. The JYTHONPATH variable can be supplemented with the additional directory:

```
export JYTHONPATH=$JYTHONPATH:/home/oracle/scripts
```

Similar to how the EM CLI Jython module was imported into the script with the command from emcli import *, the login script can be imported into either the interactive or scripting modes. To establish a login in interactive mode, we can simply import the module. We will then be prompted to enter the password for the user specified in the script. Listing 3-9 shows an example of using the login script in interactive mode.

Listing 3-9. Establishing a logon in interactive mode using the login module

```
[oracle ~]$ emcli
Oracle Enterprise Manager 12c EMCLI with Scripting option Version 12.1.0.3.0.
Copyright (c) 1996, 2013 Oracle Corporation and/or its affiliates. All rights reserved.

Type help() for help and exit() to get out.

emcli>import login
Enter password :  ********

emcli>
```

To establish a login in scripting mode, import the module from within the script being executed. For example, the following script prints the total count of Enterprise Manager targets using an EM CLI function. But first it needs to establish a login by importing the `login` module, as shown in Listing 3-10:

Listing 3-10. Establishing a login in scripting mode using the login module

```
import emcli
import login

mytargets = str(len(emcli.get_targets().out()['data']))

print(mytargets)
```

Task: Get a List of Targets

Viewing and manipulating Enterprise Manager targets are the most common uses of EM CLI. Regardless of which you are doing, the first step is to retrieve the target information.

The `get_targets` verb or function retrieves a target list along with a number of other columns of information. Neither the verb nor function requires parameters to retrieve the full list of information, as shown in Listing 3-11.

Listing 3-11. Retrieve the target information using command-line mode

```
[oracle ~]$ emcli login -username=sysman
Enter password :

Login successful

[oracle ~]$ emcli get_targets
Status  Status       Target Type      Target Name            ID
1       Up           host             oem.example.com
1       Up           oracle_emd       oem.example.com:3872
-9      n/a          oracle_home      common12c1_20_oem
```

The targets that are retrieved can be filtered by specifying a semi-colon-delimited list of target names and target types, which should be separated by a colon. There should be no white space anywhere within the target list filter. Listing 3-12 shows an example of creating a filter with two targets.

Listing 3-12. Limit the targets retrieved by `get_targets` using the `targets` parameter

```
[oracle ~]$ emcli get_targets \
   -targets='oem.example.com:host;oms12c1_3_oem:oracle_home'
Status  Status       Target Type      Target Name            ID
1       Up           host             oem.example.com
-9      n/a          oracle_home      oms12c1_3_oem
```

The `targets` parameter can use wild cards anywhere within the target name or target type values, and multiple wild cards can be used for either value, as shown in Listing 3-13.

Listing 3-13. Use wildcards in the targets parameter

```
[oracle ~]$ emcli get_targets \
   -targets='oem%:host;oms12c1_%_oem:%oracle%'
Status  Status    Target Type    Target Name            ID
1       Up        host           oem.example.com
-9      n/a       oracle_home    oms12c1_3_oem
```

Python functions require a specific format: function name, followed by an opening parenthesis, followed by a comma-delimited list of parameters and their values, followed by a closing parenthesis.

Following is an example of a typical python function:

```
function_name(parameter1=value1, parameter2=value2)
```

Since the EM CLI verbs in interactive and scripting modes are actually Python functions, they will need to follow this format as well.

Calling a function without additional parameters only requires the verb and a pair of parentheses. Listing 3-14 shows the results of using the get_targets function in interactive mode without parameters while Listing 3-15 shows the same function in scripting mode with the targets parameter.

Listing 3-14. Call the get_targets() function in interactive mode without parameters

```
[oracle ~]$ emcli
Oracle Enterprise Manager 12c EMCLI with Scripting option Version 12.1.0.3.0.
Copyright (c) 1996, 2013 Oracle Corporation and/or its affiliates. All rights reserved.

Type help() for help and exit() to get out.

emcli>import login
Enter password : ********

emcli>get_targets()
Status  Status    Target Type    Target Name            ID
1       Up        host           oem.example.com
1       Up        oracle_emd     oem.example.com:3872
-9      n/a       oracle_home    common12c1_20_oem
```

Listing 3-15. Call the get_targets() function in scripting mode with the targets parameter

```
[oracle ~]$ cat targets2.py
import emcli
import login

mytargets = emcli.get_targets \
    (targets='oraoem1%:%;oms12c1_%_oraoem1:%oracle%') \
    .out()['data']

for targ in mytargets:
    print('Target: ' + targ['Target Name'])
```

```
[oracle ~]$ emcli @targets2.py
Target: oraoem1.example.com
Target: oraoem1.example.com:3872
Target: oms12c1_3_oraoem1
```

Task: Using Blackouts

Attempting to schedule blackouts to coincide with maintenance tasks on a target host can produce false-positive alerts. This can happen when a blackout finishes prior to a maintenance activity or when a maintenance activity starts prior to a blackout. Both of these scenarios can be avoided by having the maintenance job itself start and stop the blackout.

Both EMCTL and EM CLI are capable of creating, deleting, starting, and stopping blackouts. However, EMCTL is only capable of managing blackouts for the targets local to the agent host from which it is executed, and EMCTL commands will only work if the agent is running. The limitations of setting blackouts with EMCTL are restrictive and prone to error. It is recommended to use EM CLI to set blackouts from maintenance jobs.

It is usually not necessary to use scripting mode for blackout activities since most maintenance scripts run in a shell script. The create_blackout verb requires four arguments: name, add_targets, schedule and reason. The job is identified by the name parameter, which means it must be unique to all other jobs in EM. Listing 3-16 shows an example of using EM CLI in command-line mode to set a blackout called "Blackout1" for the " em12cr3.example.com" host. This blackout will not repeat and will last for three hours or until it is stopped. The reason the blackout has been set is for "Testing."

Listing 3-16. Set a blackout called "Blackout1" for the "em12cr3.example.com" host

```
[oracle ~]$ emcli create_blackout -name='Blackout1' \
-add_targets='em12cr3.example.com:host' \
-schedule='frequency:once;duration:3' \
-reason='Testing'
```

The get_blackouts verb will show the details of all of the blackouts that are currently defined, as shown in Listing 3-17.

Listing 3-17. List all blackouts

```
[oracle ~]$ emcli get_blackouts
Name        Created By  Status      Status ID  Next Start            Duration  Reason   Frequency
Blackout1   SYSMAN      Scheduled   0          2435-07-24  17:17:56  03:00     Testing  once

Repeat  Start Time            End Time               Previous  End  TZ Region        TZ Offset
none    2000-07-24  17:17:56  2000-07-24  20:17:56   none           America/Chicago  +00:00
```

The following example uses the noheader and script parameters to change the output of get_blackouts to be easily parsed. Piping the output to the cut command displays only the first field, which is the blackout name field.

```
[oracle ~]$ emcli get_blackouts -noheader -script | cut -f1
Blackout1
```

The blackout job details can be queried with the get_blackout_details verb. The output includes a header and is tab delimited. If the output lines are longer than the screen width, they are wrapped to the next line, as shown in Listing 3-18.

Listing 3-18. List the details of the "Blackout1" blackout

```
[oracle ~]$ emcli get_blackout_details -name='Blackout1'
Status    Status ID  Run Jobs  Next Start              Duration  Reason   Frequency  Repeat  Days
Started   4          no        2014-04-12  13:37:28    03:00     Testing  once       none    none

Months  Start Time            End Time              TZ Region        TZ Offset
none    2014-04-12  13:37:28  2014-04-12  16:37:28  America/Chicago  +00:00
```

The format above is hard to read and even harder to parse. Instead, the output could be changed to a comma-delimited format, the header removed, and the output limited only to the columns we need, as shown in Listing 3-19.

Listing 3-19. List the details of the "Blackout1" blackout in a format that is easier to parse

```
[oracle ~]$ emcli get_blackout_details \
-name='Blackout1' -noheader -format="name:csv"
 Started,4,no,2014-04-12 13:37:28,03:00,Testing,once,none,none,none,2014-04-12 13:37:28,
2014-04-12 16:37:28,America/Chicago,+00:00
```

Once the output can be parsed, we can just test for the value we are looking for by adding the commands to a shell script, creating the "Blackout1" target, as shown in Listing 3-20.

Listing 3-20. Create a blackout in a script and test the exit value

```
emcli create_blackout -name='Blackout1' -add_targets='em12cr3.example.com:host'
-schedule='frequency:once;duration:3' -reason='Testing'

MYSTATUS=$(emcli get_blackout_details -name='Blackout1' \
-noheader -format='name:csv' | cut -d ',' -f 1)

if [ "$MYSTATUS" <> "Started" ]; then
echo 'Blackout not started'
        exit 1
fi

<Maintenance Script>
```

By using the above in your scripts, you would notice that after multiple runs it would sometimes fail and sometimes succeed. This behavior happens because the create_blackout EM CLI verb creates but does not start the job. The job is started by another process, so there is a chance that the blackout has not started by the time the if statement that checks the status of the job has executed, and thus the script will fail. A solution is to use additional shell scripting, which will either wait for the job to start before proceeding to the rest of the script or will fail because the job stayed in "Scheduled" mode for too long, as shown in Listing 3-21.

Listing 3-21. Additional shell scripting added to make events sequential

```
MYSTATUS='Scheduled'
STATCOUNT=6

while [ "$MYSTATUS" == "Scheduled" ]; do
        if [ $STATCOUNT -lt 1 ]; then
            echo "Blackout1 stuck in scheduled status"
                exit 1
        fi

        let STATCOUNT-=1
        sleep 5
        MYSTATUS=$(emcli get_blackout_details -name='Blackout1' \
                -noheader -format='name:csv' | cut -d ',' -f 1)
done

if [ "$MYSTATUS" != "Started" ]; then
        echo 'Blackout Blackout1 not started'
        exit 1
fi

<Maintenance Script>
```

When maintenance is completed, the same script can use EM CLI commands to both close and delete the blackout:

```
emcli stop_blackout -name='Blackout1'
emcli delete_blackout -name='Blackout1'
```

Task: Create Targets

Adding targets can be painful if EM doesn't auto-discover them. This is especially true if the targets are using non-default settings, which sometimes make them hard for the agent to detect. Fortunately, EM CLI is able to add targets with much more flexibility than EM.

Which parameters need to be specified greatly depends on the target type being added. For example, when adding a database, the properties parameter needs to include:

- SID

- Port

- OracleHome

- MachineName

The credentials for a database are almost always going to be for the "dbsnmp" user unless they are for a standby database that is not open and therefore requires a privileged password file account. Listing 3-22 shows an example of adding a target through EM CLI command-line mode.

Listing 3-22. Add the "orcl" single-instance database target

```
[oracle ~]$ emcli add_target -name='ORCL_DB' \
-type='oracle_database' -host='oradb1.example.com' \
-properties='SID:orcl;Port:1521;OracleHome:/u01/app/oracle/product/12.1.0/dbhome_1;
MachineName:oradb1-vip.example.com' \
-credentials='Role:NORMAL;UserName:DBSNMP;password:<password>'
Target "ORCL_DB:oracle_database" added successfully
```

If we want to add an RAC database target, the individual instances of the cluster need to be added first, as shown in Listings 3-23 and 3-24.

Listing 3-23. Add RAC database node one

```
[oracle ~]$ emcli add_target -name='ORCL1_ORCL_RACCLUSTER'\
-type='oracle_database' -host='oradb1.example.com' \
-properties='SID:orclrac1;Port:1521;OracleHome:/u01/app/oracle/product/12.1.0/dbhome_1;
MachineName:oradb1-vip.example.com' \
-credentials='Role:NORMAL;UserName:DBSNMP;password:<password>'
Target "ORCL1_ORCL_RACCLUSTER:oracle_database" added successfully
```

Listing 3-24. Add RAC database node two

```
[oracle ~]$ emcli add_target -name='ORCL2_ORCL_RACCLUSTER'\
-type='oracle_database' -host='oradb2.example.com' \
-properties='SID:orclrac2;Port:1521;OracleHome:/u01/app/oracle/product/12.1.0/dbhome_1;
MachineName:oradb2-vip.example.com' \
-credentials='Role:NORMAL;UserName:DBSNMP;password:<password>'
Target "ORCL2_ORCL_RACCLUSTER:oracle_database" added successfully
```

Once the instances are added, the database cluster target can be added, specifying the instances as part of the properties of the EM CLI command. These instances then become associated with the database cluster target.

___

■ **Note** Because we are adding a cluster target, a Cluster ware target must already exist before adding database cluster targets, as shown in Listing 3-25.

___

Listing 3-25. Add RAC database cluster, associating the two previous database instances

```
[oracle ~]$ emcli add_target -name='ORCL_RACCLUSTER' \
-host='oradb1.example.com' -monitor_mode='1' \
-type='rac_database' -properties='ServiceName:orclrac;ClusterName:oradb-cluster' \
-instances='ORCL1_ORCL_RACCLUSTER:oracle_database;ORCL2_ORCL_RACCLUSTER:oracle_database'
Target "ORCL_RACCLUSTER:rac_database" added successfully
```

One can use EM CLI to add almost any target type. The auto-discovery tool in EM will accurately detect most targets, making it easy to promote those targets. When an environment has customized configurations that make the auto-discovery mechanism unreliable, adding targets manually is the only option. In some environments, scripting the process of adding targets can be used to migrate between versions or to replicate an environment. In these circumstances, using EM CLI to add targets becomes a necessity.

The add_target verb accepts over a dozen parameters; use the help functionality of EM CLI for a quick reference. The online documentation provides a much more detailed description. Use the following reference if the command help isn't enough:

http://docs.oracle.com/cd/E24628_01/em.121/e17786/cli_verb_ref.htm#CACHFHCA.

My Oracle Support (MOS) also has dozens of articles on specific use cases and examples for EM CLI. MOS notes 1448276.1 and1543773.1 offer specific information on using EM CLI to add targets.

Task: Manipulating Jobs

Jobs are very important in EM. There are a number of jobs that are already created and running in a default installation. Many administrators use EM's robust job scheduling and execution capabilities for their critical enterprise tasks.

These capabilities can be fully exploited in both the GUI and EM CLI. For example, the GUI has a button called "Create Like" in the jobs library that allows one to replicate the settings from one job to another in order to reduce the amount of input necessary for two similar jobs. This functionality works great for a few jobs that look exactly alike except for one or two changes.

But what if you need to create dozens or hundreds of jobs that are similar? Or you need to replicate a number of jobs from one EM installation to another? EM CLI's functionality of exporting jobs to a text file and then importing jobs from the same file or a modified version of that file makes job manipulation at any scale possible.

For example, a simple job that executes the uname -a OS command can be exported to a file. The command and job name can be changed to uname with a different flag. Then, the modified text file with the new variables can be used to create a new job, as shown in Listing 3-26.

Listing 3-26. Describe the UNAME_A_OMS job

```
[oracle ~]$ emcli describe_job -name='UNAME_A_OMS'

# Current status of the job is EXPIRED.
name=UNAME_A_OMS
type=OSCommand
owner=SYSMAN

target_list=oraoem1.example.com:host

# Credential Usage: defaultHostCred
# Description:
cred.defaultHostCred.<all_targets>:host=SET:HostCredsNormal

# Description: (Optional) Comma separated list of parameters to the command.
variable.args=/bin/uname -a

# Description: (Optional) Command to run on the target.
variable.command=%job_default_shell%

schedule.frequency=IMMEDIATE
```

The output from this command can be used as a property file to create a new job.

1. Copy the text into a file and modify the variables as necessary (Listing 3-27).

2. To save a step, use the shell capabilities to redirect standard output to a file.

3. Copy the file just created to a new file and open that new file in a standard text editor (Listing 3-27).

4. Change the job name and command in the new file to reflect the new job (changes are shown in bold; Listing 3-28).

Listing 3-27. Create the uname_a_oms.job job properties file and make a copy

```
[oracle ~]$ emcli describe_job -name='UNAME_A_OMS' > uname_a_oms.job
[oracle ~]$ cp uname_a_oms.job uname_r_oms.job
```

Listing 3-28. Create the uname_r_oms.job job properties file

```
[oracle ~]$ cat uname_r_oms.job

# Current status of the job is EXPIRED.
name=UNAME_R_OMS
type=OSCommand
owner=SYSMAN

target_list=oraoem1.example.com:host

# Credential Usage: defaultHostCred
# Description:
cred.defaultHostCred.<all_targets>:host=SET:HostCredsNormal

# Description: (Optional) Comma separated list of parameters to the command.
variable.args=/bin/uname -r

# Description: (Optional) Command to run on the target.
variable.command=%job_default_shell%

schedule.frequency=IMMEDIATE
```

Create the new job, specifying the new properties file as the input file, as shown here:

```
[oracle ~]$ emcli create_job -input_file='property_file:uname_r_oms.job'
Creation of job "UNAME_R_OMS" was successful.
```

The UNAME_R_OMS job is now an active job. The same process can be used to create a job in the library by specifying the describe_library_job verb:

```
[oracle ~]$ emcli describe_library_job -name='UNAME_A'> uname_a.job
[oracle ~]$ cp uname_a.job uname_r.job
```

Edit the uname_r.job file. Listing 3-29 shows the contents of the script and uses the create_library_job verb to create the library job from the script.

Listing 3-29. Create the uname_a.job and uname_r.job library job properties files

```
[oracle ~]$ cat uname_r.job

# Current status of the job is ACTIVE.
name=UNAME_R
type=OSCommand
owner=SYSMAN
kind=library

# Credential Usage: defaultHostCred
# Description:
cred.defaultHostCred.<all_targets>:host=SET:HostCredsNormal

# Description: (Optional) Comma separated list of parameters to the command.
variable.args=/bin/uname -r

# Description: (Optional) Command to run on the target.
variable.command=%job_default_shell%

schedule.frequency=IMMEDIATE

[oracle ~]$ emcli create_library_job -input_file='property_file:uname_r.job'
Creation of library job "UNAME_R" was successful.
```

Exporting jobs gives one the ability to easily duplicate jobs (both active and library), as well as to keep an external backup of that job in a generic format. This backup can serve as a method of restoring the job to another system, building a duplicate or test system, and producing an audit record if necessary.

Summary

The terminology of EM CLI can be confusing for someone who is not a regular user. Verbs define the functionality of what you want to do with EM CLI. The "flavors" of how you make changes with EM CLI are known as modes. Command-line mode is also known as classic mode, where one command is executed at a time. Interactive and scripting modes use Python syntax and can additionally use the mature functionality of that powerful programming language.

Given its size and complexity, it is impossible for someone to memorize everything about EM CLI. Even the most advanced user will need the assistance of documentation on a regular basis. Fortunately, EM CLI is loaded with help. From the excellent documentation found online to the manual pages contained within the command-line and interactive modes of the tool itself, all of the information one needs is easily and readily available.

No one likes an error message, but when they pop up in EM CLI, they are descriptive and usually easy to read and interpret. The syntax of errors in many products can be tricky, especially with all of the different tools administrators have to switch between on a daily basis. The error syntax in EM CLI is intuitive and simple when compared to many of those other tools.

EM CLI will already be fully configured and ready to use on each installed OMS. It is also easy to download, install, and set up on any other machine that is capable of running Java. The method of communication between the EM CLI client and the OMS is almost identical to the communication that takes place between the browser and the OMS. Both are highly secure and use standard, mature technologies.

However, EMCTL is not going away any time soon. Despite the fact that EMCTL and EM CLI can do some of the same things, they are vastly different in their purposes and functionality. Try not to make the mistake of dismissing EMCTL as futile because of the robustness of EM CLI. You will need them both for different tasks.

The examples in this chapter show just a small sliver of what EM CLI can do, but chances are, you already have in mind a few scenarios where EM CLI can solve a problem that the GUI and other command-line tools cannot. The examples here are some of the most obvious ways to use EM CLI. There are multiple ways and tools by which to solve most problems in Enterprise Manager. The examples shown in this book will never claim to be the "right" way to do something. Use the information found here to come up with your own "right" way.

▪ ▪ ▪

## CHAPTER 4

Working at the Command Line

EM CLI is ideally suited for shell scripts, but it also simplifies tasks that are ordinarily performed in the console. For instance, removing an EM agent and its related targets through the console can be quite trying. With EM CLI, you issue a one-line command and the same tasks execute quickly and completely from the command line.

This chapter will introduce you to some of the basics of EM CLI at the command line and then illustrate several ways you can apply EM CLI to administering your environment more quickly—without all the mouse clicks required to perform the same tasks in the console.

We often associate the term "command line" with Unix, and that's applicable here too, but do remember that since EM CLI is a Java application it can be run on any platform. EM CLI runs the same whether you're logged into a server or executing the commands from your desktop.

Start an EM CLI Session

Although each CLI command is run on a separate line, when logging into EM CLI a single session is established for all subsequent statements. The login verb establishes a connection to the OMS server and validates the user before any work starts. You may either enter your password on the command line (not recommended for interactive sessions) or wait to be prompted for the password during the login process.

The sync command ensures that your run-time execution uses the current verb definitions available in the management server's software library. This is particularly important after you've patched or upgraded your OMS.

```
emcli login -username="SYSMAN"

emcli sync
```

CLI References

Oracle document #E17786.12 contains a catalog of the EM CLI verbs available with the release of OEM 12.1.0.4. Check with Oracle at http://docs.oracle.com/cd/E24628_01/em.121/e17786.pdf to make sure you have the latest version.

Help is also available online through EM CLI itself. The current listing of verbs known to your OMS software library is available at the command line.

```
emcli help

> emcli help

Summary of commands:   argfile    -- Execute emcli verbs from a file
    help        -- Get help for emcli verbs (Usage: emcli help [verb_name])
    login       -- Login to the EM Management Server (OMS)
    logout      -- Logout from the EM Management Server
    setup       -- Setup emcli to work with an EM Management Server
    status      -- List emcli configuration details
    sync        -- Synchronize with the EM Management Server
    version     -- List emcli verb versions or the emcli client version

  Add Host Verbs
    continue_add_host          -- Continue a failed Add Host session
    get_add_host_status        -- Displays the latest status of an Add Host session.
    list_add_host_platforms    -- Lists the platforms on which the Add Host operation can be
                                  performed.
    list_add_host_sessions     -- Lists all the Add Host sessions.
    retry_add_host             -- Retry a failed Add Host session
    submit_add_host            -- Submits an Add Host session.

  Agent Administration Verbs
    get_agent_properties    -- Displays details of all properties of an agent
    get_agent_property      -- Displays the value of specific property of an agent
    resecure_agent          -- Resecure an agent
    restart_agent           -- Restart an agent
    secure_agent            -- Secure an agent
    set_agent_property      -- Modify specific property of an agent
    start_agent             -- Start an agent
    stop_agent              -- Shut down an agent
    unsecure_agent          -- Unsecure an agent
...
```

Add the name of a verb to the help command for specific guidance on that verb. The example below shows the help result for the sync verb.

```
> emcli help sync
  emcli sync

  Description:
    Synchronize the emcli client with the OMS.

    After synchronization, all verbs and associated online help
    available to that OMS become available at the emcli client.
    Synchronization automatically happens during a call to a setup.
  Options:
    -url
        The URL of the EM (OMS).
        Both http and https protocols are supported
        (https is recommended for security reasons).
```

```
 -username
     The EM username to be used by all subsequent emcli commands
     when contacting the OMS.
 -password
     The EM user's password.
     If this option is not specified, the user is prompted
     for the password interactively.
     Providing a password on the command line is insecure and
     should be avoided.
 -trustall
     Automatically accept any server certificate from the OMS,
     which results in lower security.
     Also indicates that the setup directory is local and trusted.
```

The get_targets Verb

EM CLI verbs fall into three broad categories: EM queries, OEM administrative actions, and target manipulations. Verbs use a very specific syntax, so the names of targets being passed to EM CLI must match the object's name in OEM's dictionary.

The get_targets verb can be used to verify the target name prior to its use in any administrative or maintenance task. For instance, let's say you want to create a blackout for database orcl1 on host myhostx and that you promote discovered database and listener targets through the automated process. The database target in OEM may have been added as sidc_myhostx, by its RAC instance name, or perhaps by its global name. Sometimes it may even appear as its service name or SID. This variability can occur when you use target promotion through Auto Discovery Results. You should set target names manually when you add targets, using the guided discovery process to ensure consistency across your enterprise.

Output Formats

EM CLI has three preconfigured output formats for query results. User-defined formats are also supported.

- *Pretty* format aligns the column headings with the result-set data.

- *Script* format separates the values in the heading and results columns with a space. This format works very well with the awk programming language.

- *Csv* format, as the name suggest, separates the values with a comma for parsing in a spreadsheet or with the shell's cut command.

Let's say you want to set the OEM credentials for the eamz database using this command:

```
emcli set_credential -target_type=oracle_database -target_name="eamz" \
                -credential_set=DBCredsNormal \
                -columns="username:dbsnmp;password:Super_S3cret;role:Normal"
```

Your command would fail because OEM can't find a matching target name. Figure 4-1 illustrates the different styles.

```
emcli get_targets -targets="oracle_database" -format="name:csv" | grep -i eamz
```

```
>emcli get_targets -targets="oracle_database" -format="name:pretty"
Status    Status                Target Type          Target Name
 ID
1         Up                    oracle_database      eamzgr
1         Up                    oracle_database      eamzg
1         Up                    oracle_database      tolv
1         Up                    oracle_database      gold
1         Up                    oracle_database      eamz.world
>
>emcli get_targets -targets="oracle_database" -format="name:script"
Status ID         Status  Target Type       Target Name
1          Up     oracle_database eamzgr
1          Up     oracle_database eamzg
1          Up     oracle_database tolv
1          Up     oracle_database gold
1          Up     oracle_database eamz.world
>
>emcli get_targets -targets="oracle_database" -format="name:csv"
Status ID,Status,Target Type,Target Name
1,Up,oracle_database,eamzgr
1,Up,oracle_database,eamzg
1,Up,oracle_database,tolv
1,Up,oracle_database,gold
1,Up,oracle_database,eamz.world
```

Figure 4-1. *Output style samples*

We'll explore several examples of applying this verb later in this chapter as well as in the next.

Agent Administration

The ability to install the EM CLI client on your desktop allows you to execute an EM CLI command without opening a browser—no need to use the console or log into the management server host. This flexibility allows you to quickly control the OEM agents using one of the many EM CLI verbs related to them.

As we saw earlier, you can use the get_targets verb to find the specific name of any agent by filtering the get_targets results for target type oracle_emd. This is particularly important for agents, since the agent name contains the host name and port number.

```
> emcli  get_targets -targets="oracle_emd"  -name="name:csv"
Status ID,Status,Target Type,Target Name
1,Up,oracle_emd,acme_dev:2480
1,Up,oracle_emd,acme_qa:3872
1,Up,oracle_emd,acme_prod:3872
```

The targets variable also accepts paired values that include the target name and target type, like this: -targets="acme_qa:oracle_database"

All of the agent-management tasks available through the OEM console are also available as EM CLI verbs. Notice in these examples that the password is required for the OEM agent binary owner/host user in every case.

```
emcli stop_agent  -agent=acme_qa:3872 -host_username=oracle
Host User password:
The Shut Down operation is in progress for the Agent: acme_qa:3872
The Agent "acme_qa:3872" has been stopped successfully.
```

```
emcli start_agent  -agent=acme_qa:3872 -host_username=oracle
Host User password:
The Start Up operation is in progress for the Agent: acme_qa:3872
The Agent "acme_qa:3872" has been started successfully.
```

```
emcli restart_agent  -agent=acme_qa:3872 -host_username=oracle
Host User password:
The Restart operation is in progress for the Agent: acme_qa:3872
The Agent "acme_qa:3872" has been restarted successfully.
```

Agents sometimes fall out of sync with the OMS after patching or as a result of an outage and thus require an update to their registration information or even an agent synchronization in order to permit uploads. The easiest way to achieve this is to resecure the agent to straighten out the connection. If your environment does not require secured agents, you can remove the secure relationship by executing the unsecure_agent verb with identical syntax to the secure_agent verb.

Notice that the password for the owner of the agent executable and the OMS registration password are both required.

```
emcli secure_agent  -agent=acme_qa:3872 -host_username=oracle
Host User password:
Registration Password:
The Secure operation is in progress for the Agent: acme_qa:3872
The Agent "acme_qa:3872" has been secured successfully.
```

```
emcli resecure_agent  -agent=acme_qa:3872 -host_username=oracle
Host User password:
Registration Password:
The Resecure operation is in progress for the Agent: acme_qa:3872
The Agent "acme_qa:3872" has been resecured successfully.
```

The agent_resync verb kicks off a job in the repository database to update the status of a blocked agent. An agent is placed in blocked status when the repository contains conflicting data from the agent upload. This typically happens after unscheduled issues affect the agent connection to the OMS. As a result, standard output isn't informative at the command line. While you can click through to the job in the console to track the progress, there is no matching option in EM CLI.

```
emcli resyncAgent -agent=acme_qa:3872
Resync job RESYNC_20140422135854 successfully submitted
```

EM CLI can also be used to provide detailed information about an agent, either listing all of its properties or drilling down to a specific property, as shown below.

```
emcli get_agent_properties -agent_name=acme_qa:3872
Name                        Value
agentVersion                12.1.0.3.0
agentTZRegion               America/Los_Angeles
emdRoot                     /opt/oracle/agent12c/core/12.1.0.3.0
agentStateDir               /opt/oracle/agent12c/agent_inst
perlBin                     /opt/oracle/agent12c/core/12.1.0.3.0/perl/bin
scriptsDir                  /opt/oracle/agent12c/core/12.1.0.3.0/sysman/admin/ scripts
EMD_URL                     https://acme_qa:3872/emd/main/
REPOSITORY_URL              https://myoms.com:4903/empbs/upload
EMAGENT_PERL_TRACE_LEVEL    INFO
UploadInterval              15
Total Properties :          10

emcli get_agent_property -agent_name=acme_qa:3872 -name=agentTZRegion
Property Name: agentTZRegion
Property Value: America/Los_Angeles
```

Deleting EM Targets with EM CLI

The delete_targets verb can be used to remove individual targets or a group of related targets. It may seem simpler to select targets individually from the console and press the Delete Target button. That's usually true, but we've found that under some conditions it's possible to end up with orphaned targets, like an oracle_dbsys target type left behind when all its fellow members were deleted. Besides, if you have an EM CLI client installed on your desktop you can remove the target without logging into the console!

Let's first look at an example of removing an individual target. Let's say that database bertha was finally retired, and so was the related listener LSNRBERTHA. Both of them belong to an oracle_dbsys target type.[1]

Find Exact Target Names

The console derives target names and target types from session information, so target deletion within the console is sure to use the exact name and target type for both of these targets. To find those values, we'll use the get_targets verb and a simple grep to distinguish the targets we're interested in.

```
> emcli get_targets | grep -i bertha
1       Up          oracle_database    bertha
1       Up          oracle_dbsys        bertha_sys
1       Up          oracle_listener       LSNRBERTHA_oemdemo.com
```

Delete the Target

The database and listener both belong to the database system bertha_sys, so all three can be deleted with one command:

```
> emcli delete_target -type = "oracle_db_sys" -name="bertha_sys" -delete_members
  Target "bertha_sys:oracle_dbsys" deleted successfully
```

---

[1]There are several target types in your environment. During its installation, the EM agent discovers the targets on the host and associates them with specific target types. A new Oracle Home is created and the appropriate plug-in is installed for each target type identified. The labels of each target type are fixed, and each target is associated with one and only one target type.

You can also delete individual members, like this:

```
> emcli delete_target -type = "oracle_listener" -name="LSNRBERTHA"
  Target "LSNRBERTHA:oracle_listener" deleted successfully
```

How to Remove an Enterprise Manager Agent with One Command

Removing an EM agent from Enterprise Manager requires removal of all the targets managed by that agent and all of their metrics. In the console, this requires multiple deletion actions in roughly reverse order of their discovery. For instance, when you first deploy an agent to a host, the agent and host become the first and second targets known. Then you discover and promote other targets residing on the host.

Monitored targets are removed in the reverse order of discovery so that referential data can be removed properly from the repository database. Target removal must start with the discovered/promoted targets, then the host, and finally the agent.

The delete_targets verb removes the agent and its monitored targets in just one command if you use the delete_monitored_targets flag.

```
> emcli delete_target -name="<Agent Name>"
  -type="oracle_emd"
  -delete_monitored_targets
  -async;
```

■ **Note**   The agent must be stopped prior to deletion.

The process for deleting the agent target type is very similar to that for removing other target types. Since agent names consist of the host name and agent port number, we'll run get_targets first.

```
> emcli get_targets | grep -i demohost01
1       Up          host                    demohost01
1       Up          oracle_emd              demohost01:3872

> emcli delete_target -name="demohost01:3872" -type="oracle_emd" -delete_monitored_targets -async;
Target "LSNRBERTHA:oracle_listener" deleted successfully
```

Complete removal of the agent involves activities on the management server (OMS) as well as work on the remote host. See Table 4-1.

Table 4-1. *Agent Removal Tasks*

Location	Action	Example
Remote host	Get the target name from the agent	`> emctl status agent	grep "<Agent URL>"`
Remote host	Stop the agent with emcli or emctl. You could also use emcli stop_agent verb described earlier in this chapter to shut it down from a CLI session. Since the complete agent-removal task includes on OUI session on the remote host, as in this case it is simpler to execute the emctl command	`> emctl stop agent`

OMS	Delete the target	`> emcli delete_target -name="<Agent Name>"`
		 `  -type="oracle_emd"`
		 `  -delete_monitored_targets`
		 `  -async;`

Remote host	Uninstall plugin and sbin binaries. OUI Oracle home removal carries the same relationships as target creation inside OEM. The agent home was created first and must be deleted last in a separate step.	`cd $AGENT_BASE/core/<agent release>/oui/bin` `./runInstaller -deinstall –remove_all_files`
Remote host	Uninstall the agent software with the including_files option	

Transferring Targets to Another EM Agent

Changes happen. Perhaps you've decided to move a database to a different host or you want to change the directory containing your EM agent binaries. You could drop and rediscover the targets, but you'd lose their metric history.

You can retain that history and reassign metric collection and blackout responsibility for specific targets to another EM agent using the `relocate_targets` verb.

How It Works

Each EM agent has its own targets.xml file located in $AGENT_BASE/agent_inst/sysman/emd. The `relocate_targets` verb updates those XML files on the source and destination hosts and also updates the relationships in the repository.

The agent and the targets it monitors must reside on the same host. That means that you can't use `relocate_targets` to monitor databases through an agent on a different host. This technique is limited to moving targets to an EM agent on the same host or to performing a migration task to another server. Let's look at an example.

To move goldfish database and its listener from the alice server to buster:

```
emcli relocate_targets
  -src_agent="alice:3872"
  -dest_agent="buster:3872"
  -target_name="goldfish"
  -target_type="oracle_database"
  -copy_from_src

emcli relocate_targets
  -src_agent="alice:3872"
  -dest_agent="buster:3872"
  -target_name="lsnrgoldfish"
  -target_type="oracle_listener"
```

For the transfer you'd use these values:

- src_agent= alice:3872   (current agent name)
- dest_agent= buster:3872 (destination agent name)
- target_name= goldfish   (name of the target to move)
- target_type= EM types for that target

Database targets also include the copy_from_src flag in order to retain their history. You can only relocate one target per EM CLI command.

OMS-Mediated Targets

Do not use the relocate targets verb with RAC databases or Oracle clusters of any type. Your management server knows about the relationships between clustered objects that use Oracle software and will mediate agent responsibilities automatically across the clustered hosts. If you manually relocate a clustered target to another agent in another cluster you run the risk of corrupting OEM's associations between the cluster members.

You can query the repository database to determine which targets are OMS mediated as follows:

```
SELECT    entity_type,
          entity_name,
          host_name
FROM      sysman.em_manageable_entities
WHERE     manage_status =2-- Managed
AND       promote_status =3-- Promoted
AND       monitoring_mode =1-- OMS mediated
ORDERBY   entity_type,entity_name, host_name;
```

ENTITY_TYPE	ENTITY_NAME	HOST_NAME
cluster	clust01	cluster01b.com
cluster	clust01	cluster01b.com
rac_database	apple	cluster01b.com
rac_database	betty	cluster01a.com
rac_database	jack	cluster01b.com
weblogic_domain	/EMGC_GCDomain/GCDom	myoms.com
weblogic_domain	/Farm01_IDMDomain/ID	myoms.com
weblogic_domain	/Farm02_IDMDomain/ID	myoms.com

Managing OEM Administrators

The console provides a clear, convenient method for managing OEM administrator accounts, but its flexibility makes it tremendously inconvenient for creating multiple accounts as you click through all the screens. EM CLI combines the flexibility inherent in the OEM codebase with the simplicity of the command-line interface.

All of the options defined in the console can be granted as options in EM CLI using the flags shown below. To create an administrator you only need to give the account a name and password.

```
emcli create_user -name="SuzyQueue" -password="oracle"
```

You wouldn't be reading a book from Apress if you were one to ignore user security, so you'll want to expire the user's new password with the -expired="true" flag, like this:

```
emcli create_user -name="SuzyQueue" -password="oracle" -expired="true"
```

Other optional parameters allow you to perform most of the user grants available in the OEM console but without the click-stream. Both EM CLI and the OMS server use the same codebase, so this should come as no surprise.

Role Management

Enterprise Manager administrators and users are stored as database user accounts in the repository database. Resist the temptation to grant role privileges through SQL*Plus, since there may be other actions being performed by OEM's internal security management.

You can add role grants while creating the user by adding the -roles parameter:

```
emcli create_user -name="SuzyQueue" -password="oracle" \
                            -roles="em_all_administrator"
```

You can also modify the user through the grant_roles or revoke_roles verbs:

```
emcli grant_roles -name="SuzyQueue" -roles="em_all_viewer"
```

```
emcli revoke_roles -name="SuzyQueue" -roles="em_all_operator"
```

We'll discover how to build out a set of administrators using shell scripts in the next chapter.

Tracking Management Server Login

Occasionally you may want to know who is logged in to your management servers. The list_active_sessions verb provides that information with details if you pass the –details flag, like this:

```
emcli list_active_sessions -details
```

```
OMS Name: myoms.com:4889_Management_Service
Administrator: SYSMAN
Logged in from: Browser@123.45.6.234
Session: F7CA6D7DE88B0917E04312E7510A9E54
Login Time: 2014-04-24 06:46:53.876687
```

```
OMS Name: myoms.com:4889_Management_Service
Administrator: BOBBY
Logged in from: Browser@SAMPLEPC.com
Session: F7CD5C7EE0A961C7E04312E7510A8A71
Login Time: 2014-04-24 11:05:24.199258

OMS Name: myoms.com:4889_Management_Service
Administrator: PHIL
Logged in from: Browser@123.45.6.228
Session: F7CECDD6335543E3E04312E7510AA25C
Login Time: 2014-04-24 11:13:20.567234

OMS Name: myoms.com:4889_Management_Service
Administrator: SYSMAN
Logged in from: Browser@123.45.6.234
Session: F7CF52CA3BE1692FE04312E7510A7494
Login Time: 2014-04-24 11:50:31.152683

OMS Name: myoms.com:4889_Management_Service
Administrator: SYSMAN
Logged in from: EMCLI@123.45.6.231
Session: F7CF52CA3BE3692FE04312E7510A7494
Login Time: 2014-04-24 11:55:52.482938

OMS Name: myoms.com:4889_Management_Service
Administrator: SYSMAN
Logged in from: Browser@123.45.6.231
Session: F7CF52CA3BE5692FE04312E7510A7494
Login Time: 2014-04-24 12:07:52.335728
```

Summary

EM CLI allows you to perform many administrative tasks from the command line and even on your desktop. The simple techniques described in this chapter lend themselves handily to shell scripting and further automation, as described in the following chapter.

## CHAPTER 5

Automation Through Shell Scripts

As we discovered in the previous chapter, EM CLI provides faster means of accomplishing complicated tasks that are ordinarily managed through the OEM console. The strength of EM CLI is leveraged by combining EM CLI with classic shell-scripting techniques. The examples in this chapter are written for use in a Unix/Linux environment but, because EM CLI is a Java application, the CLI syntax shown here will work just as well in other environments.

This chapter begins with CLI scripting fundamentals and then works through several examples demonstrating application of the technique. In each example, we've removed the common housekeeping commands that make scripts robust in order to ensure our illustrations are clear. Since those techniques apply to any scripted solution, we'll lay out some fundamental scripting guidelines before tackling any OEM solutions.

All the examples in this chapter are written using fundamental bash shell scripts due to their ubiquity and clarity. Perl or other languages can be applied to improve script performance, but adding that element to this chapter could mask the basics of the techniques being demonstrated.

This chapter begins by laying out some shell-scripting fundamentals and advances to building and applying shell functions. Along the way we'll take a look at how to create and control OEM blackouts, manage user accounts, and work with larger data sets. Finally, we'll take a look at some advanced shell-scripting techniques using getopts.

Best Practices for Shell Scripting

Everyone with experience in shell scripting, whether for Windows, Linux, or any other Unix variant, has their own preferred techniques. Hopefully, the scripts in your environment present a consistent look and feel that makes it easy to read and easy to maintain. Best practices for writing any program, regardless of shell or operating system, were laid out by the creators of Unix and documented in *The Art of Unix Programming* by Eric S. Raymond. Those guidelines provide a very clear foundation for any programming we perform. A free online copy of the book is available at https://archive.org/details/ost-computer-science-the_art_of_unix_programming.

Logging

Mysteries belong on your night stand and not in your Enterprise Manager environment. Output for any Unix program should provide useful, complete, and concise screen output at run-time along with thorough log files. Log files are created through the redirection of the shell output.

Redirection

Echo statements direct their standard output to the screen. This type of output was one of the earliest capabilities for the Unix operating system and makes log-file creation a simple extension of the scripts. One can redirect output using either one or two elbows (also referred to as chevrons or angle brackets), typically pointed to the right. A simple echo statement sends standard output to the screen.

```
echo "Hello world"
Hello world
```

You can redirect that same output directly to a file with a right elbow:

```
echo "Hello world"> myFile.lst

cat myFile.lst
Hello world
```

Single right elbows create a new file, while double right elbows append output to a file.

```
echo "Shell scripting makes me hungry">> myFile.lst
echo "What about you?">> myFile.lst

cat myFile.lst
Hello world
Shell scripting makes me hungry
What about you?
```

Robust shell scripts are written both for unattended scheduled activities (cron, for instance) and for interactive execution for debugging and one-off use. "Piping to a tee" allows immediate feedback at the console and also writes standard output to a file, like this:

```
echo "Hello world"| tee myFile.lst
Hello world

cat myFile.lst
Hello world
```

Append to files by tacking -a onto your tee statement:

```
echo "Shell scripting makes me hungry"| tee -a myFile.lst
echo "What about you?"| tee -a myFile.lst
```

Error Handling

Even the simplest Unix program expects that your program will make the machine do the work. Poorly written scripts make assumptions based on, and perhaps tested against, existing installations and configurations. As you well know, nothing stays the same in our business, so program for the unexpected.

Nothing is as frustrating as a program that fails-out when it discovers a problem that it could easily be handled by the script. For instance, if your script requires a specific directory for logs or staging then the script should create those directories and set the proper permissions required by your program:

```
if [ ! -d /tmp/staging ]; then
      mkdir -p /tmp/staging
      chmod 770 /tmp/staging
fi
```

Hung program execution is another area in which your program should anticipate failures and test for problem situations before they happen. For example, empty files can cause your script to hang, so before grepping file output, you should check to see that the file truly exists:

```
if [ -f myFile.lst ]; then
  cat myFile.lst | grep "Hello World"
else
  echo "File myFile.lst is missing!"
  exit 1
fi
```

There are several other relevant scripting guidelines in *The Art of Unix Programming*. The examples we just considered are representative of the types of programming fundamentals omitted from this chapter in the interest of brevity and clarity.

Passwords and Shell Scripts

Among all the guidelines and suggestions for shell programming there has always been one hard and fast rule: Never hard-code passwords into your scripts—it can become a maintenance and security nightmare. It is up to you to develop a method for managing your password files. The choice is yours whether you develop an in-house Java solution, apply a technique you found on the web, depend on obfuscation and hidden files, or use some other bit of cleverness. It is beyond the scope of this book to suggest solutions.

The remainder of this chapter will use the variable named ${SECRET_PASSWORD} whenever a password is required in the script.

Calling EM CLI from a Shell Script

Command-line utilities like SQL*Plus run in a subshell inside of shell scripts, wrapped in "Here Documents" that are typically shown as opening and closing EOF tags, like this example shows:

```
sqlplus / as sysdba <<EOF
  SELECT sysdate FROM dual;
  exit
EOF

SYSDATE
---------
03-AUG-14
```

You can find more information about this process at http://www.tldp.org/LDP/abs/html/here-docs.html

Each EM CLI command runs on a stand-alone statement, so a subshell is not required when called by your shell script. In its place, you should use shell script functions when a series of related CLI commands needs to be executed together.

Shell Script Functions

Shell function syntax is quite simple. Just follow these steps:

1. Using the keyword function, give the function a name followed by an opening brace. Braces are the curly brackets { }, and brackets are these angular objects: [ ].

2. Include the shell commands to be executed.

3. Add a closing brace.

In the following example, the contents of several directories are copied to a backup destination. The code for creating the file list and the actions required to move the files could be repeated for each directory. Instead, the recurring tasks are performed by the same block of code, which is called by the function name CopyFiles. Common supplemental tasks, such as compressing and chmodding the files, can be added so as to function for single-source editing.

Variables, such as SOURCE_DIR, TARGET_DIR, and WORKFILE, are passed to the function at run-time. Dependent variables, such as SOURCE_FILE and TARGET_FILE, are populated at run-time for each directory:

```
# ----------------------------------------------------
# Functions
# ----------------------------------------------------
function CopyFiles {
cd $SOURCE_DIR

ls -l | grep -i $ORACLE_SID      >$WORKFILE

for thisFILE in `cat $WORKFILE`; do
   SOURCE_FILE=$SOURCE_DIR/$thisFILE
   TARGET_FILE=$TARGET_DIR/$thisFILE
   cp -f $SOURCE_FILE $TARGET_FILE
done

rm -f $WORKFILE
}

# ----------------------------------------------------
# Run-time Procedure
# ----------------------------------------------------
SOURCE_DIR=/gold_scripts/rman
TARGET_DIR=/test_scripts/rman
   CopyFiles

SOURCE_DIR=/gold_scripts/security
TARGET_DIR=/test_scripts/security
   CopyFiles
```

As we saw in the last chapter, each EM CLI session begins with two commands—login and sync. This same practice should be followed when starting a session in a script. You could repeat the same sequence each time your script starts a CLI session, like this:

```
emcli login -username="SYSMAN"-password=${
emcli sync
```

Since these two commands always execute together, they form the basis for a simple shell script function, seen below. We'll look at some more-complex functions later in the chapter.

```
function EmcliLogin {
        emcli login -username="SYSMAN" -password="${SECRET_PASSWORD}"
        emcli sync
}
```

GetTargetName Function

In the previous chapter we explained how the get_targets verb can be used to determine the exact name of an OEM target. Since shell scripts are built to handle edge cases, like missing directories, any target-manipulation script should verify the following:

1. The target exists in OEM.

2. You use the exact name of the target in your CLI command.

Build the get_targets verb into a function by giving it a name and wrapping the commands in braces. In this example the value for INPUT_VAL is passed into the function by the calling script:

```
function GetTargetName {
if [ `emcli get_targets | grep ${INPUT_VAL}%"| grep oracle_database" |  wc -l` -gt 0 ];
then
        thisTARGET=`emcli get_targets -format -name="name:csv"| grep -i ${INPUT_VAL} | grep
oracle_database | cut -d, -f4`
        echo "Target name is ${thisTARGET}"
else
        echo "No matching targets found"
fi
}
```

In this example, we set a variable named thisTARGET for the exact target name known to OEM for the Oracle database acme_qa. At run-time, the target name will be passed from the command line or through additional scripting (working through a list of targets, for instance). The steps outlined here are explained in detail later.

1. Determine first whether a matching target exists.

2. If it does exist, set the variable thisTARGET to match and announce your success. Logging and interactive user communication are essential to troubleshooting shell scripts. Share the status whenever new information is available at run-time.

3. If it does not exist, fail loudly and politely. One of the core Unix programming rules is that programs should fail as early as possible and loudly as possible. Shell scripts are no exception.

Filtering and parsing to determine the final variable string runs through this sequence:

1. Get a list of all targets of a type with oracle% in the name.

2. Grep that list for targets matching acme_qa.

3. Grep that shorter list for oracle_databases.

4. Cut the list by delimiting on the comma and returning the fourth value.

Step 1: List of all targets with "oracle%" in their name

```
Status ID,Status,Target Type,Target Name
1,Up,oracle_emd,acme_dev:3872
1,Up,oracle_emd,acme_qa:2480
1,Up,oracle_emd,acme_prod:3872
1,Up,oracle_database,amce_dev
1,Up,oracle_database,acme_qa
1,Up,oracle_database,acme_prod
1,Up,oracle_listener,lsnracmedev
1,Up,oracle_listener,lsnracmeqa
1,Up,oracle_listener,lsnracmeprod
```

Step 2: Filter that list for strings containing acme_qa

```
1,Up,oracle_database,acme_qa
1,Up,oracle_listener,lsnracmeqa
```

Step 3: Just list the database

```
1,Up,oracle_database,acme_qa
```

Step 4: Return the fourth string after a comma delimiter

```
acme_qa
```

Be sure to call the function by name during script execution:

```
read INPUT_VAL?"Enter the database to be managed:"
GetTargetName
```

Managing Blackouts with EM CLI

The most common use of Enterprise Manager is to send notifications for target down events or metrics that fall outside limits you've set. You control those alerts during planned outages by creating blackouts for individual targets or groups of targets. There are a number of settings required to create a blackout, and the EM console provides a handy, attractive means to do it.

EM CLI provides a means of creating, stopping, and deleting blackouts inside your shell scripts. All of the same options found in the console are configurable through EM CLI, since it exercises the same Java code behind the scenes.

You must provide three values for the EM CLIcreate_blackout verb.

- Unique name for each blackout passed as -name
- Targets to include in the blackout, used in -add_targets argument
- Schedule information about start and end times,input as -schedule argument

The-reason variableis not required by EM CLI but should be included to make it easier for OEM administrators to assess running, scheduled, and stopped blackouts. Be courteous.

The syntax to create a simple blackout is fairly straightforward:

```
> emcli create blackout -name="sample_blackout"\
-add_targets="oracla:oracle_database"\
-schedule="duration::360 ..."
-reason="Blackout demonstration using emcli"
```

Name Argument

You may pass anything as the name of a blackout. The blackout name is applied when you create the blackout, but it's also used when it's time to stop and delete the blackout. It's always a good practice to use a descriptive name like scripted_blackout_$SID or a similar, consistent naming standard. As we work through the examples, you'll begin to see how consistency affects your solution's design.

Add Targets Argument

Targets must be identified by target name and target type. For example:

- oracla:oracle_database
- demohost:host
- lsnroracla:oracle_listener

Schedule Argument

Each schedule argument accepts two required and several optional values at the command line, similar to the flexibility found in the console:

frequency:once

```
requires => duration or end_time
optional => start_time, tzinfo, tzoffset
```

frequency:interval

```
requires => duration, repeat
```

optional => start_time, end_time, tzinfo, tzoffset

```
frequency:weekly
requires => duration, days
optional => start_time, end_time, tzinfo, tzoffset
frequency:monthly
requires => duration, days
optional => start_time, end_time, tzinfo, tzoffset
```

```
frequency:yearly
requires => duration, days, months
optional => start_time, end_time, tzinfo, tzoffset
```

A Robust Solution for Scheduled Blackouts

The author's environment contains a handful of application training databases that get refreshed from a cold backup nightly. Of course, as soon as these targets were added to OEM he started getting pager notifications at night caused by these planned outages. You can imagine his reaction.

- The simplest solution is to blackout these targets all night on a schedule in the console.

- What if you need to run this refresh during the day?

- Do you really want these targets to be unmonitored overnight?

- What if the refresh failed? Trainers are not typically patient customers, particularly with a roomful of idle trainees waiting for their lab.

Here's a solution that involves shell functions, EM CLI, and their related run-time scripts. We'll start by taking a look at how the process would typically be done without shell functions, and then we will convert the script into portable, scalable functions.

Create and Stop Blackouts Using Shell Scripts

Blackouts can be created through a series of CLI verbs to perform the following steps to test, execute, and then verify the blackout status.

1. Determine whether the target is already under blackout.

2. If a blackout already exists, stop and delete it (to get the full duration of your new blackout).

3. Create and start a new blackout.

4. Verify that the blackout is started by echoing its values to the screen and also to the log file.

These steps are illustrated in this simplified script. Your real script would test whether the database name was passed as the $1 value at the command line and would then prompt or fail based on run-time conditions. For instance, if the script is being executed by a live user, it should prompt for the database name, otherwise it will fail and echo the cause to the logfile.

```
#!/bin/ti
# ======================================================
# File:        create_blackout.sh
# Purpose:     Create and initiate an OEM blackout
# Parameters:  Blackout name as BO_NAME
# ======================================================
export BO_NAME=${1}_scripted_blackout

echo  "\n\nCreating blackout named '${BO_NAME}' ...\n"
```

```
if [ `emcli get_blackouts | grep ${BO_NAME} | wc -l` -gt 0 ]; then
        $ECHO "\n\nFound an existing blackout named ${BO_NAME}"
        $ECHO "That blackout will be stopped and deleted prior to starting the new one\n\n"
        emcli stop_blackout -name="${BO_NAME}"
        emcli delete_blackout -name="${BO_NAME}"
fi

emcli create_blackout
-name="${BO_NAME}"
        -add_targets="${thisTARGET}:oracle_database"
-schedule="duration::360"
-reason="Scripted blackout for maintenance or refresh"

sleep 5

echo "\n\nGetting blackout information for '${BO_NAME}' ...\n\n"
emcli get_blackout_details -name="${BO_NAME}"
```

There are several things to notice in this short script:

- Each blackout name must be unique, so this script requires some portion of the name to be passed at the command line. In this example we pass the SID.

- User communication is important anytime, so be complete and be concise. Your echo's statements are useful at run-time and essential in the log file.

- This planned blackout will run six hours (duration:360) maximum, so you want to delete an existing blackout of the same name to get all six hours.

- Notice that the stop_blackout and delete_blackout verbs take the blackout name as their only input value. You must stop a blackout before you can delete it.

- The test for blackout status is important for the run-time log file.

In practice, this appears as a series of wrap-around entries in the crontab, like this:

```
25 19 * * * /scripts/oem/create_blackout.sh gold
30 19 * * * /scripts/refresh/restore_training.sh gold
30 20 * * * /scripts/oem/end_blackout.sh gold
```

When you start a blackout you should also plan on stopping it. This side of the scripted pair is simpler, of course, because there is a lot less to do:

```
#!/bin/sh
# =====================================================
# File:       end_blackout.sh
# Purpose:    End an OEM blackout
# Parameters: Blackout name as BO_NAME
# =====================================================
export BO_NAME=${1}_scripted_blackout
echo  "\n\nStopping blackout named '${BO_NAME}' ...\n"
if [ `emcli get_blackouts | grep ${BO_NAME} | wc -l` -gt 0 ]; then
        $ECHO "\n\nFound an existing blackout named ${BO_NAME}"
        emcli stop_blackout -name="${BO_NAME}"
        emcli delete_blackout -name="${BO_NAME}"
fi
```

Creating and Using a Function Library

The previous example assumes that everything goes well with the refresh and that OEM resumes monitoring after an hour. Of course, the blackout will end six hours after it starts, even without end_blackout.sh. Why not turn off the blackout right after the work is done?

Converting this activity to shell functions in a central library allows you to start and stop the blackout inside the restore_training.sh script, as shown here:

```
#!/bin/sh
# =======================================================
# File:        restore_training.sh
# Purpose:     Refresh database from a cold backup copy of datafiles
# Parameters:  Database name as ORASID
# =======================================================
# Source the OEM function library
. /script/oem/emcli_functions.lib

export BO_NAME=database_refresh_${ORASID}

CreateBlackout

< Existing your in-house database restoration commands >

EndBlackout
```

Only one cron entry (or OEM scheduled job) is required because you've wrapped the work of all three scripts into one wrapper.

The function library sourced in this example contains the functions CreateBlackout and EndBlackout. The function library is simply a non-executable text file stored in a central location on each server, preferably through NFS mounts or a similar shared file system.

This snippet only contains the two functions relevant to this example. Chapter 8 contains an example of a complete function library. Your production CLI function library can contain many others, in addition to these two. Notice that the contents of the functions are identical to the code we used in the separate shell scripts. They're just recorded as functions.

```
# =======================================================
# File:    emcli_functions.lib
# Purpose: Shared function library for EM CLI scripts
# Note :   Source this library to load its contents into memory
# =======================================================
function CreateBlackout {
echo "\n\nCreating blackout named '${BO_NAME}' ...\n"

if [ `emcli get_blackouts | grep ${BO_NAME} | wc -l` -gt 0 ]; then
echo "\n\nFound an existing blackout named ${BO_NAME}"
        echo "That blackout will be stopped and deleted prior to starting the new one\n\n"
        emcli stop_blackout -name="${BO_NAME}"
        emcli delete_blackout -name="${BO_NAME}"
fi
```

```
emcli create_blackout -name="${BO_NAME}"
 -add_targets=${thisTARGET}:oracle_database
 -schedule="duration::360;tzinfo:specified;tzregion:America/Los_Angeles"
 -reason="Scripted blackout for maintenance or refresh"
}

function EndBlackout {

echo "\n\nStopping blackout '${BO_NAME}' ...\n"
emcli stop_blackout -name="${BO_NAME}"

echo "\n\nDeleting blackout '${BO_NAME}' ...\n"
emcli delete_blackout -name="${BO_NAME}"
}
```

Once the library is created, you're free to leverage these same functions across all of your scripts, even at the command line. For instance, let's say you need to blackout the databases on a particular server for operating system patches. At the command, you'd source the function library and then call the functions as needed. Files are sourced by typing a period, a space, and then the file name. For instance, when you log into a Unix/Linux server, your user profile will source the .bashrc and .bash_profile (if Bash is your shell of choice) to load your environment variables into memory. When you type the env command, it will reflect those values. Sourcing other files, like a function library, loads paths, values, functions, or aliases from the new file into memory to supplement or replace the environment variables already in place:

```
. /script/oem/emcli_functions.lib
for thisSID in suzie, sally, betty, veronica; do
    BO_NAME=os_patch_blackout_${thisSID}
    echo "Starting the blackout for ${thisSID}"
    CreateBlackout ${BO_NAME}
done
```

You'd reverse this using a similar process when the work is done:

```
. /script/oem/emcli_functions.lib
for thisSID in suzie, sally, betty, veronica; do
    BO_NAME=os_patch_blackout_${thisSID}
    EndBlackout ${BO_NAME}
done
```

In addition to the simplicity of your run-time environment, either at the command line or in a script, you can be assured that the code in the function library has been tested in other use cases. The function library also removes opportunities for mistyped commands and forgotten steps.

EMCTL or EMCLI

Enterprise Manager control utility, or EMCTL, is installed with each OEM agent and is used to manually start and stop OEM agents and to manage local functionality at the remote host.

EMCTL can be used to start and stop (but not delete) OEM blackouts just like EM CLI, but with one key advantage: EMCTL is already installed and configured. If you choose EM CLI as your blackout-management tool for a remote host using shell scripts, you must manually install and configure the EM CLI client on each host. EM CLI client is a static installation of a Java program. The client software installations are reported but not managed through OEM itself. The number of remote hosts in your environment might make EMCTL the better solution if you are limiting the functionality to blackout maintenance and other tasks that it can manage. The installation process covered in Chapter 2 provides a scripted means of performing that installation.

Managing blackouts with EMCTL is very similar to the techniques used for EM CLI and lends itself to the same scripting applications.

The syntax is straightforward:

```
emctl start blackout <blackout name><target names>
emctl start blackout <blackout name>  -nodelevel
emctl stop blackout <blackout name>
emctl status blackout <blackout name>
```

The nodelevel flag blacks out all targets on the node and works well for patching activities.

Durations are specified by a –d flag and may be set for a combination of days and hours like this:

```
emctl start blackout WeekendBlackout  -nodelevel –d 2 12:00
```

In this example, a blackout for all targets on a development node could be scheduled to start at 6:00 PM on a Friday and would run up to 6:00 AM on Monday (two days and twelve hours).

Managing OEM Administrators with EM CLI

The console provides a clear, convenient method for managing OEM administrator accounts, but its flexibility makes it tremendously inconvenient for creating multiple accounts as you click through all the screens. By the author's count, creating a new administrator in the console requires at least 17 mouse clicks! EM CLI combines the flexibility inherent in the OEM code base with the simplicity of the command-line interface.

All of the options defined in the console can be granted as options in EM CLI using the flags shown below. To create an administrator you only need to give the account a name and password:

```
emcli create_user -name="SuzyQueue"-password="oracle"
```

You wouldn't be reading a book from Apress if you ignored user security, so you'll want to expire the user's new password with the -expired="true" flag, like this:

```
emcli create_user \
  -name="SuzyQueue"\
  -password="oracle"\
  -expired="true"
```

The other optional parameters allow you to perform the user grants available in the OEM console but without the click-stream.

Role Management

Enterprise Manager administrators and users are actually database user accounts in the repository database. Resist the temptation to grant role privileges through SQL*Plus, since there may be other actions performed by OEM in account management.

You can add role grants while creating the user by adding the -rolesparameter:

```
emcli create_user \
  -name="SuzyQueue"\
  -password="oracle"\
  -roles="em_all_administrator"
```

You can also modify the user through the grant_roles or revoke_roles verbs:

```
emcli grant_roles \
  -name="SuzyQueue"\
-roles="em_all_viewer"

emcli revoke_roles \
  -name="SuzyQueue"\
  -roles="em_all_operator"
```

Batch Processing with Argfile

EM CLI has a batch-processing verb named argfile that, like many other Oracle parfiles, allows you to execute multiple commands in a single EM CLI execution by providing a fully qualified path in the text file containing the input values to be applied.

For example, let's load up a text called /tmp/create_several_users.lst with the CLI required to create a few users:

```
touch /tmp/create_several_users.lst
for thisADMIN in Sugar Magnolia Blossom Blooming, do
    echo "create_user -name=${thisADMIN} -password=oracle -expired=true";
done

cat /tmp/create_several_users.lst
create_user -name="Sugar"-password="oracle"-expired="true"
create_user -name="Magnolia"-password="oracle"-expired="true"
create_user -name="Blossom"-password="oracle"-expired="true"
create_user -name="Blooming"-password="oracle"-expired="true"

emcli login -username=SYSMAN -password="${SECRET_PASSWORD}"
emcli sync
emcli argfile "/tmp/create_several_users.lst"
```

The following are advantages of using an argfile:

- The EM CLI utility is invoked outside the argfile, so verbs are processed serially without restarting EM CLI.

- An argfile is a text file, and your choice of suffix has no bearing at all on execution. The example has an lst suffix but you could just as easily use cli or cmd.

- You must fully qualify the path to the argfile.

- This example does not include file cleanup, but I'm sure your script will.

As you might suspect, this method is quite efficient, and argfile executions typically run very fast since there is a single call to the OMS through the CLI utility.

Populating an Argfile from a Text File

Creating and editing an argfile by hand isn't out of the question, but sometimes (always?) a scripted solution is easier and less error prone. For instance, what if you received a request to provide OEM access to several members of an application group with the following CSV file attached?

■ **Note**   Backslashes are included for clarity in this illustration. Put each complete string on one line.

```
cat manage_request.txt
login,name,department,email e123450,"Jerry",A100,jerry@samplecorp.com
e123451,"Bobby",A100,bobby@samplecorp.dom
e123452,"Phil",A100,phil@samplecorp.dom
e123449,"Robert",A100,roberth@samplecorp.dom
e123499,"Ron",A100,ronpig@samplecorp.dom
e123460,"Bill",A110,bill@samplecorp.dom
e123461,"Mickey",A110,mickey@samplecorp.dom
e123491,"Keith",A120,keith@samplecorp.dom
e123492,"Donna",A120,donnaj@samplecorp.dom
e123460,"Brent",A120,brent@samplecorp.dom
```

We'll redirect output from a loop statement to create the argfile, like this:

```
touch /tmp/user_builder_argfile.lst

for thisENTRY in `cat manage_request.txt`; do
  LOGIN=`echo ${thisENTRY} | cut -d, -f1`
  NAME=`echo ${thisENTRY} | cut -d, -f2`
  DEPT=`echo ${thisENTRY} | cut -d, -f3`
  EMAIL=`echo ${thisENTRY} | cut -d, -f4`
echo "delete_user -name=${NAME} \n >>/tmp/user_builder_argfile.lst
echo "create_user -name=${NAME} \
\t -password=oracle -expired=true \
    \t -desc=${NAME} \
    \t -department=${DEPT} \
    \t -email=${EMAIL} \
    \t -roles="EM_USER \n"
```

```
>>/tmp/user_builder_argfile.lst
done
echo "\n\nArgfile has been created\n"
cat /tmp/user_builder_argfile.lst
```

We end up with an argfile that looks like this:

```
delete_user -name=e123450
create_user -name=e123450 -password=oracle -expired=true \
-desc=Jerry -department=A100 -email=jerry@samplecorp.com-roles=EM_USER
delete_user -name=e123451
create_user -name=e123451 -password=oracle -expired=true \
-desc=Bobby -department=A100 -email=bobby@samplecorp.com-roles=EM_USER
. . .
```

At run-time we'll see this:

```
>emcli argfile /tmp/user_builder_argfile.lst
>User "e123450"deleted successfully
>User "e123450"created successfully
>User "e123451"deleted successfully
>User "e123451"created successfully
...
```

It's fast and efficient because all of the commands are issued to the OMS in one CLI session, reducing the overhead of sending each command to the OMS for processing as a separate transaction.

Cloning OEM Roles and Users Between OMS Instances

Sandbox OEM servers are part of a well-designed OEM environment, but copying EM security data from one repository to another can be difficult without EM CLI. This example combines SQL*Plus and EM CLI to gather data from the existing environment and then reproduce it in the sandbox quickly and completely.

First, we'll create three spool files from queries against the SYSMAN schema in the existing OEM repository database. Those spool files will become the EM CLI argfiles we'll use to build the roles, users, and grants.

The SYSMAN schema in the repository database contains all the information gathered or set by OEM. When the EM agents upload their latest metrics to the management server, the values are posted to tables in the SYSMAN schema. Whenever you request a page in the console it is populated from data in SYSMAN.

```
#!/bin/bash# =======================================================
#  File:         clone_em_users.sh
#  Purpose:      Copy OEM roles and user account between instances
#  Parameters : None
#  ========================================================
ARGFILE01=/tmp/argfile_create_roles.txt
ARGFILE02=/tmp/argfile_create_users.txt
ARGFILE03=/tmp/argfile_grant_roles.txt
```

```
sqlplus -S ${SYSMAN_CONNECT} <<EOF 1>/dev/null
SET ECHO OFF
SET FEEDBACK OFF HEADING OFF LINES 250 PAGES 999

SPOOL ${ARGFILE01}

SELECT 'create_role -name="' || role_name || '" -description="' || description || '"'
FROM      sysman.gc_roles
WHERE   role_type= '1';

SPOOL OFF

SPOOL ${ARGFILE02}

SELECT    'create_user -name="' || user_name || '" -description="' || user_description ||
'" -password='||oracle||
"  -expired="||true||'"'
FROM      sysman.gc_users
WHERE   user_name NOT IN ('SYSMAN')
ORDER BY user_name;

SPOOL OFF

SPOOL ${ARGFILE03}

SELECT 'grant_roles -name="' || user_name || '" -roles="' || role_name || '"'
FROM      sysman.gc_user_roles;

SPOOL OFF
exit
EOF

emcli login -user=sysman -pass=${CONSOLE_PWD}
emcli -argfile ${ARGFILE01}
emcli -argfile ${ARGFILE02}
emcli -argfile ${ARGFILE03}
```

Changing EM Administrator References

As we mentioned in the previous section, all of the information you create through OEM is stored in the repository database. User data for OEM accounts is stored in the sysman.mgmt_created_users table. You should never directly change data in the repository, of course, but you may use it as reference data.

Updating an individual administrator is simple and straightforward through the EM console. However, what if the name of department changed or a group of administrators changed locations?

You could create a short script to change the references when everyone in department 200 gets assigned to department 500 by gathering a list of employees in department 200 into a spool file and then rolling through each line in the spool file to create modify_user statements for each one. The script consists of a combination of SQL and EM CLI commands. Right now there are no CLI verbs to gather this information directly, so we'll pull it from the repository.

Many of the error-checking routines typical when prompting for user input have been removed for clarity: Did the user provide answers? Were the department numbers entered in upper or lower case? Are they valid numbers? Scalable and reliable scripts must always include those verifications.

```
#!/bin/bash
# =================================================================
# File:          change_admin_depts.sh
# Purpose:       Change department number references for EM admins
# Parameters:    None
# =================================================================
read OLD_DEPT?"Enter the old department number:  "
read NEW_DEPT?"Now enter the new department number: "

sqlplus <Connect String><<EOF
SET echo OFF
SET heading OFF feedback OFF page 999
spool old_department.lst
SELECT user_name
FROM    sysman.mgmt_created_users
WHERE   department = '${OLD_DEPT}';
spool off
exit
EOF

touch myARGFILE.lst

for thisUSER in `cat old_department.lst`; do
        echo "modify_user -name="${thisUSER}"-department="${NEW_DEPT}">>myARGILE.lst
done

emcli argfile myARGFILE.lst

echo "\n\nDepartment settings after the change:\n"
sqlplus <Connect String><<EOF
SET echo OFF
SET heading ON pages 999
SELECT user_name,
       department
FROM   sysman.mgmt_created_users
ORDER BY user_name;
exit
EOF
[ old_department.lst ] && rm -f old.department.lst
[ myARGFILE.lst ] && rm -f myARGFILE.lst
```

The last two steps clean up the temporary files created at run-time. Every shell script should clean up after itself. The syntax above checks for the existence of the file and removes it when one is found. You could also build a simple if statement if you choose.

Shell Getopts Command

In addition to getopts (plural), Linux has a getopt (singular) command. This discussion is about getopts. This is a shell utility, not an EM CLI verb. The previous example prompted the user for two department numbers, which is fine for interactive scripts but isn't scalable for scheduled jobs. You could use positional parameters at the command line, like this:

```
if [ $1 ]; then
export OLD_DEPT=${1}
else
read OLD_DEPT?"Enter the old department number:   "
fi

if [ $2 ]; then
        export NEW_DEPT=${1}
else
read NEW_DEPT?"Enter the new department number:   "
fi

if [[ ${OLD_DEPT} == ${NEW_DEPT} ]]; then
        echo "The values for the old and new departments are the same"
        < Error handling >
fi
```

This approach relies on user inputs being presented in the correct order. In the current example, the first input value corresponds to the old department and the second to the new department. What if they aren't in the right order, however? The getopts command allows you to use input flags to avoid this problem.

Command-line input is evaluated by a case statement in your script that determines how flag values are to be handled. The order they were entered on the command line is irrelevant. OPTARG is the name of the value passed by getopts. Let's look at how that works. For this entry on the command line, a string will be returned via the getopts output named OPTARG.

```
./change_admin_depts.sh -a 500 -b 750

while getopts a:b: OptValue; do
  case $OptValue in
    a) export OLD_DEPT=${OPTARG};;
    b) export NEW_DEPT=${OPTARG};;
    *) echo "No values were provided for old and new departments";;
  esac
done
```

This example tested a temporary variable named OptValue against expected characters and responded accordingly. Each value identified as an -a or -b on the command line set corresponds to a value for a new or old department number.

```
echo $OLD_DEPT
500
echo $NEW_DEPT
750
```

Values identified by a character followed by a colon ":" in the getopts statement indicate that the flag will be followed by a string. An OptValue without a colon won't accept a string and can be used to signal a particular process in your script.

In the example below, if the -t flag is received on the command line, a function named RunTestFunctions is executed:

```
change_admin_depts.sh -a 747 -b 757 -t
```

The script handles each of these requests in order:

```
while getopts a:b:t OptValue; do
  case $OptValue in
    a) export OLD_DEPT=${OPTARG};;
    b) export NEW_DEPT=${OPTARG};;
    t) export TestOnly="True"
    *) echo "No values were provided for old and new departments";;
  esac
done


if [ $TestOnly == True ]; then
RunTestFunctions
fi
```

The flexibility of this approach grows with the number of values you can handle. For instance, the logic in the ChangeAdminDepts function could be adapted to process the other values you can set with the modify_user verb, like line of business and location. The getopts flags could be used to determine which of those functions to apply. See the example below:

```
while getopts a:b:t OptValue; do
  case $OptValue in
    a) export OLD_DEPT=${OPTARG};;
    b) export NEW_DEPT=${OPTARG};;
    c) export OLD_LOB=${OPTARG};;
    d) export NEW_LOB=${OPTARG};;
    e) export OLD_LOCATION=${OPTARG};;
    f) export NEW_LOCATION=${OPTARG};;
    t) export TestOnly="True"
    *) echo "No values were provided for old and new departments";;
  esac
done

if [ ${#OLD_DEPT} -gt 0 ]; then
        if [ ${#NEW_DEPT} -gt 0 ]; then
ChangeAdminDepts
else
        echo "Error: You provided the old department but"
        echo "the value for the new department is missing."
        echo "Please run this script again and provide"
    echo "both values when prompted"
        exit 1
fi
fi
```

Updating Target Properties Using Argfile

OEM properties provide another data point for targets and administrators. For instance, setting the Department property for host and database targets could be useful for filtered reports, or you could use a property to map targets to administrators. The Lifecycle Status property can be used to filter up-time reports. You get the idea. It's another reference point outside of built-in OEM structures like Groups.

Despite their usefulness, it's fairly inconvenient to set properties for an OEM target. When you discover a new host or configure a connection to a new database, you aren't prompted for LifeCycle Status, Department, Location, or any of the other properties that are directly assignable to a target in the console.

As a result, some of your targets may not have current or accurate values in those fields. Here's a query that uses string logic to derive LifeCycle Status from the host name. In this example, production hosts are named oraprod01, oraprod02, etc. Test and development hosts enjoy the same common naming standards. Note: Naming standards like this flash a signal to hackers saying "Don't waste your time on that dev/test server—all my production data is over here!" This is just an example.

The set_target_property_value verb allows you to set a single property for a single target. You have better things to do, so we'll pull those verb strings into an argfile by loading the results of that query into a SQL spool file, like this:

```
sqlplus -S ${SYSMAN_CONNECT} <<EOF SET ECHO OFF
SET FEEDBACK OFF HEADING OFF LINES 250 PAGES 999
SPOOL ${ARGFILE01}
SELECT
        CASE SUBSTR ( host_name, 0, 6 )
            WHEN 'oraprod' THEN
             DECODE ( property_value, 'Production', NULL, 'set target_property_value
-property_records="' || target_name ||':oracle_database:LifeCycle Status:Production"' )
            WHEN 'oratest' THEN
             DECODE ( property_value,'Test', NULL,'set_target_property_value -property_records="' ||
target_name ||':oracle_database:LifeCycle Status:Test"' )
            WHEN 'oradevl' THEN
             DECODE ( property_value,'Development', NULL,'set_target_property_value
-property_records="' || target_name ||':oracle_database:LifeCycle Status:Development"' )
        ELSE ''Not defined'
        END  AS corrective_action
FROM    sysman.gc$target_properties a,
        sysman.gc$target b
WHERE   a.target_guid = b.target_guid
 AND    b.target_type = 'oracle_database'
 AND    a.property_name = 'orcl_gtp_lifecycle_status';

SPOOL OFF
EOF

if [ `cat ${ARGFILE01} | wc -l` -gt 0 ]; then
    emcli login -user=sysman -pass=${CONSOLE_PWD} 2>/dev/null
    emcli argfile ${ARGFILE01}
    emcli logout

fi
```

Summary

EM CLI supports many of the techniques available within the console and allows you to manage and manipulate target data within portable shell scripts or OEM jobs. This chapter focused on native shell scripts, but a faster, more flexible technique for script with jython was released with release 12.1.0.3. The following chapter shows you how to leverage that capability.

The availability of advanced scripting with jython shouldn't dissuade you from fundamental shell scripting. Shell scripts run without additional installations or configurations. They also have the advantage of being familiar to nearly all administrators.

CHAPTER 6

▪▪▪

Advanced Scripting

Much of the power of a command-line interface like EM CLI is the ability to automate the execution of multiple commands at a time. This chapter dives deep into the marriage of Python and EM CLI in what is known as interactive and scripting mode.

The first part of the chapter reviews some of the history of where Python, Jython, and JSON came from. Being able to take advantage of Python functionality in EM CLI requires a basic understanding of programming and Python syntax. An introduction to Python in this chapter, including examples, will allow even the first-time Python user to tackle Python efficiently in EM CLI.

Finally, a detailed example will feature the use of a Python class object to take advantage of EM CLI functionality to modify the properties of multiple targets at a time. This is a common task that is tedious in the graphical user interface and is necessary to understand and use in EM CLI.

History of Python

Python was created in the late 1980s by Guido van Rossum and originated from an interpreted language called ABC. At the time, van Rossum was working with ABC and liked the syntax but wanted to change some of the functionality. During the Christmas holidays of 1989, van Rossum designed the language that would later be called Python. Python was officially released in 1991 while van Rossum worked for a company called Stichting Mathematisch Centrum in Amsterdam.

Python did not get its name from the dangerous reptile, but rather from the popular British BBC comedy series, *Monty Python's Flying Circus*. Van Rossum was a fan of the show and needed a name that was fitting for the language.

Van Rossum continues to have a central role and has been named Python's Benevolent Dictator for Life (BDFL). This term was coined for van Rossum but has become a common description for open-source software that has retained its creator as the final decision maker for disputes or arguments within the community.

Python is a programming language, but because the code is compiled at runtime, it can also be considered a scripting language. There is not always a clear delineation between the two, and the definition of each has changed over time. Generally, programming languages must be compiled before they can be run and scripts are run from a set of commands, either interactively or from a file. Since Python can do either and both at the same time, the answer to the question "Is Python a programming or a scripting language?" is "Yes!"

Jython

Jython is an implementation of Python written in Java. Jython was initially created in late 1997 to replace the "C" implementation of Python with Java for performance-intensive code accessed by Python programs. Knowing how to code in Java, while beneficial to working with Jython, is not a prerequisite. In fact, one can use Jython with no knowledge of Java whatsoever. However, when using Jython it is likely one will come across Java code, as Jython programs use Java classes in addition to Python modules.

The Enterprise Manager Command-Line Interface is written almost entirely in Java and Jython. The download of EM CLI from the OMS is a JAR file that requires the Java executable to install. When EM CLI is used in interactive mode, the command-line interface is Jython.

The rest of this chapter will refer to Python and Jython interchangeably. This is because most users start out with Python and subsequently learn Jython, or use only Python language (no Java) when using Jython. There is a great deal of information and tutorials for Python on the Internet and in books, so it is advised to search "Python" instead of "Jython" when looking up syntax, examples, and so forth.

If you've ever used any of Oracle's middleware products, you have likely already come across Jython. WebLogic Application Server's Scripting Tool (also known as "wlst") also uses Jython.

JSON

The output of EM CLI commands will be displayed in one of two ways. The standard tabular or columnar format is known as "text" mode. The text mode is generally the most readable form of the data up to a certain point. For example, a table with five columns displays well in text mode, but a table made up of 20 columns is very difficult to read or parse. Text mode is the default mode of display for EM CLI interactive mode.

An alternative to text mode for displaying command output is JavaScript Object Notation, commonly known as JSON. JSON was originally derived from JavaScript and has since become a universal tool for data interchange. Nearly every programming and scripting language not only uses and understands JSON, but also has a vast array of built-in functionality for it.

JSON is the default method of storing and displaying command output for the "scripting" mode of EM CLI, which was built for processing EM CLI commands and output. It is expected that the data received from the commands processed in an EM CLI script will be manipulated in some way.

Getting Started

Python was built for ease of use and brevity. For those reasons, it is not difficult for a novice to learn the basic functionality of the language and to use it to accomplish tasks. DBAs often have an advantage when it comes to learning Python because of their experience with PL/SQL, Java, shell scripting, various command-line interfaces, and analytical tendencies.

Perhaps Python's most noticeable feature is the use of indentation for block structure. Instead of using open and close statements to enclose a block of flow control, such as if statements, Python uses four spaces to indent lines of code that belong to a block. Therefore, the line above the first line not indented ends the block. The first line of the block is always followed by a colon.

```
>>> for VAR in myLoop:
...     do this command
>>> this line does not belong in the loop
```

Both Python and Jython (as well as EM CLI and WLST) have an interactive interface in which any command executed in a script can be written or copied and executed to see the results in real time. Most Linux hosts will have Python installed. To invoke the interactive interface, simply type python:

```
[root@server ~]# which python
/usr/bin/python
[root@server ~]# python
Python 2.6.6 (r266:84292, Jul 10 2013, 06:42:56)
[GCC 4.4.7 20120313 (Red Hat 4.4.7-3)] on linux2
Type "help", "copyright", "credits" or "license" for more information.
>>>print("this is the interactive Python prompt")
this is the interactive Python prompt
>>>exit()
```

Hello World!

"Hello World!" is the most common introduction to any programming or scripting language. The following example uses three lines of code to demonstrate five important concepts in Python that will be used in nearly every script. Notice the lack of extraneous text or commands in each line.

```
>>> myvar = 'Hello World!'
>>> if myvar:
...     print(myvar)
...
Hello World!
```

The first line shows how to assign a value to a variable. The variable does not need to be created before being assigned a variable. Both steps are done at once. The value assigned to myvar is a string value, making the variable a string variable.

The second line starts an if block. The block says, "If the variable myvar exists and has a value assigned to it, proceed to the next line in this block." The opening line of code blocks always ends with a colon.

The third line prints the value of the myvar variable, followed by a new line. The print function always includes a newline character at the end of the printed string.

The fourth line requires a carriage return to indicate the code block is finished. This is not the case in a script, where blank lines after code blocks are not necessary.

The fifth line shows the output of the code-block commands. This would indicate that the myvar variable did indeed exist and had a value assigned to it, so the line within the code block was executed, evidenced by the success of the print function.

Finding Help

There is myriad information available on the Internet regarding Python. A simple Internet search will return more than enough results to refresh one's memory about a forgotten command. But, Python does one better. A full suite of help is available right from the command line.

Basic syntax on how to use the internal help in Python can be read by calling the help() function, which puts the user into another command-line interface within Python where almost any keyword (including "help") found anywhere in Python can be entered to provide easy-to-understand information:

```
>>> help()

Welcome to Python 2.6!  This is the online help utility.

If this is your first time using Python, you should definitely check out
the tutorial on the Internet at http://docs.python.org/tutorial/.

Enter the name of any module, keyword, or topic to get help on writing
Python programs and using Python modules.  To quit this help utility and
return to the interpreter, just type "quit".

To get a list of available modules, keywords, or topics, type "modules",
"keywords", or "topics".  Each module also comes with a one-line summary
of what it does; to list the modules whose summaries contain a given word
such as "spam", type "modules spam".

help>
```

For example, if I need to know something about a string, I can type `string` within the `help>` command line, and then I can read about the many ways strings are used in Python. Perhaps a simpler way to find information is to look up a topic by typing `topics`. The command prints out a list of available topics, including STRINGS. Typing STRINGS presents an easy-to-understand article about strings in Python. Typing the letter q will exit the article, and typing <CTRL-D> will exit the help command line:

```
help> topics

Here is a list of available topics.  Enter any topic name to get more help.

ASSERTION            DEBUGGING           LITERALS            SEQUENCEMETHODS2
ASSIGNMENT           DELETION            LOOPING             SEQUENCES
ATTRIBUTEMETHODS     DICTIONARIES        MAPPINGMETHODS      SHIFTING
ATTRIBUTES           DICTIONARYLITERALS  MAPPINGS            SLICINGS
AUGMENTEDASSIGNMENT  DYNAMICFEATURES     METHODS             SPECIALATTRIBUTES
BACKQUOTES           ELLIPSIS            MODULES             SPECIALIDENTIFIERS
BASICMETHODS         EXCEPTIONS          NAMESPACES          SPECIALMETHODS
BINARY               EXECUTION           NONE                STRINGMETHODS
BITWISE              EXPRESSIONS         NUMBERMETHODS       STRINGS
BOOLEAN              FILES               NUMBERS             SUBSCRIPTS
CALLABLEMETHODS      FLOAT               OBJECTS             TRACEBACKS
CALLS                FORMATTING          OPERATORS           TRUTHVALUE
CLASSES              FRAMEOBJECTS        PACKAGES            TUPLELITERALS
CODEOBJECTS          FRAMES              POWER               TUPLES
COERCIONS            FUNCTIONS           PRECEDENCE          TYPEOBJECTS
COMPARISON           IDENTIFIERS         PRINTING            TYPES
COMPLEX              IMPORTING           PRIVATENAMES        UNARY
CONDITIONAL          INTEGER             RETURNING           UNICODE
CONTEXTMANAGERS      LISTLITERALS        SCOPING
CONVERSIONS          LISTS               SEQUENCEMETHODS1

help> STRINGS
String literals
***************


String literals are described by the following lexical definitions:

    stringliteral   ::= [stringprefix](shortstring | longstring)
    stringprefix    ::= "r" | "u" | "ur" | "R" | "U" | "UR" | "Ur" | "uR"
    shortstring     ::= "'" shortstringitem* "'" | '"' shortstringitem* '"'
...


:q


help> <CTRL-D>
You are now leaving help and returning to the Python interpreter.
If you want to ask for help on a particular object directly from the
interpreter, you can type "help(object)". Executing "help('string')"
has the same effect as typing a particular string at the help> prompt.
>>>
```

The help function is also very useful in EM CLI. The developers spent a lot of time making sure information is contained within the program. Unlike Python, typing help() does not drop into another command line; it simply prints out a list of verbs, sorted and grouped by category.

The individual verbs can then be specified in the help function for more detailed information on that verb. For example, typing help('list_active_sessions') in EM CLI would print out detailed information on the list_active_sessions() function.

Python Objects

An object in Python is an entity that can hold data and, in most cases, be manipulated by changing the data contained within the object or by changing the attributes of the object itself. The content and complexity of a Python object depends on the object type. For example, if you need an object with just a single digit, you would use a number object. If you need a multiple key/value object, you would use a dictionary object. The life of an object begins when it is created or assigned a value and ends when it is explicitly destroyed or when the Python session ends. This section lists the most common object types and shows examples of how to create and use them.

Numbers and Strings

A number object is an entity that contains a single integer value. A string object is an entity that contains a single string value. These types of objects are mutable, which means the assigned value can be changed or replaced at any point during the life of the object. These are by far the most commonly used objects in Python.

The "Hello World!" example introduced the most basic object in Python: the string. Strings are used everywhere in Python, and most other objects are made up of numbers and strings. Strings can include numbers, but numbers cannot include strings.

This example shows how to create a simple string object by assigning a string to a variable:

```
>>> mystring = 'Here is my string'
>>> type(mystring)
<type 'str'>
```

I can create a number object by assigning a number to a variable. int stands for integer:

```
>>> mynumber = 12345
>>> type(mynumber)
<type 'int'>
```

Numbers and strings are different types of objects. Trying to join a string value to a number value results in error:

```
>>> mystring + mynumber
Traceback (most recent call last):
  File "<stdin>", line 1, in <module>
TypeError: Can't convert 'int' object to str implicitly
```

Lists

Lists are a common way to store an indexed group of values within an object. A simple list is assigned to an object in a similar way to how a string is assigned to an object, the difference being that the object is now a list object, not a string object. The significance of this is not as great in Python as in other languages, but it is a good idea to have an understanding that there is a difference that can potentially have an impact on the behavior of a program.

This example shows a list object with a single value. The values assigned to a list are encapsulated by brackets. Without the brackets this would be a simple string object. See here:

```
>>> mylist = ['one']
>>> print(mylist)
['one']
>>> type(mylist)
<type 'list'>
>>> mystring = 'one'
>>> type(mystring)
<type 'str'>
```

Simple Lists

A list with a single value can be useful, but the purpose of lists is to be able to assign multiple list values within a single object. These values are referred to as *elements*. In the previous example, a value of one was assigned as the first element in the mylist object.

This example creates a list called mylist with five members. Printing the list displays it exactly how it was created. The five elements are printed within an opening and closing bracket. The brackets are what tell us that this is a list and not a string or any other type of object. A list index of 2 is actually the third element in the list since the index numbers start at 0.

The power of lists comes from the plethora of ways that the individual elements can be manipulated. For example, any element can be queried from a list by specifying its index number. The index of a list starts at zero, so the first element of a list is assigned the number zero:

```
>>> mylist = ['one', 'two', 'three', 'four', 'five']
>>> print(mylist)
['one', 'two', 'three', 'four', 'five']
>>> type(mylist)
<type 'list'>
>>> print(mylist[2])
three
```

A list is mutable, which means it can be manipulated after it has been created. It can be lengthened or shortened, and the elements can be changed. This example shows the mylist object being appended with the value of 6. The number of elements in this object goes from five to six:

```
>>> mylist.append('six')
>>> print(mylist)
['one', 'two', 'three', 'four', 'five', 'six']
>>> print(len(mylist))
6
```

The len() function used in the previous example displays the number of elements in the list. Like many functions, len() can be used on lists, strings, and all other object types.

The next example shows how to further manipulate a list by extracting and deleting the last element of myshortlist. The first command in this example does three things. The pop function extracts and then deletes from mylist the last element, creates the myshortlist list object, and assigns to it the "popped" element. If the pop() function weren't preceded by an object assignment, it would simply print the element:

```
>>> myshortlist = mylist.pop()
>>> print(myshortlist)
six
>>> print(mylist)
['one', 'two', 'three', 'four', 'five']
```

Lists in EM CLI

Lists play a critical role in EM CLI. The output of the functions in EM CLI may produce a list with hundreds or even thousands of elements, and those elements may be composed of strings, numbers, or other objects. The lists in EM CLI work in exactly the same way that they do in the previous examples.

Understanding everything about the following example is not important right now, but it is important to note that the list() function is one of the most-used functions in EM CLI and always returns a list object. This list has 29 elements that can be "popped" off one at a time and assigned to another object:

```
emcli>mytargs = list(resource='Targets').out()['data']
emcli>type(mytargs)
<type 'list'>
emcli>len(mytargs)
29
emcli>myshorttargs = mytargs.pop()
emcli>print(myshorttargs)
{'TYPE_DISPLAY_NAME': 'Oracle WebLogic Server', 'TYPE_QUA...
```

The output of the list EM CLI function is a list of target information.

Strings and Lists

This section will show how to accomplish the common task of finding a running Oracle database listener in Linux by using the Linux ps and grep commands. The first part of the example will show how to produce the process information. The second part of the example will show how to parse the output of the ps command using various Linux utilities, followed by the use of Python to accomplish the same task.

Listing 6-1 shows a detailed listing of an Oracle database listener background process. The ps -ef command lists all of the running processes on the server, which are piped into grep to limit the output to just the listener processes.

Listing 6-1. Find the Oracle database listener process in Linux

```
[oracle@server ]$ ps -ef | grep [t]nslsnr
oracle    1723     1  0 16:21 ?        00:00:01
/u01/app/oracle/product/12.1.0/dbhome_1/bin/tnslsnr LISTENER -inherit
```

The combination of ps and grep shows that a single listener is running and shows the full command in the eighth column of the output. The listener command actually includes two spaces, so to us it looks like the command spans the eighth, ninth, and tenth space-delimited columns. The awk command parses this information quite well, as shown in Listing 6-2.

Listing 6-2. Use **awk** to parse the process detail

```
[oracle@server ]$ ps -ef | grep [t]nslsnr | awk '{print $8,$9,$10}'
/u01/app/oracle/product/12.1.0/dbhome_1/bin/tnslsnr LISTENER -inherit
```

Listing 6-3 shows that Python would treat the output from the ps command as an object made up of pieces. The delimiter used in the previous example is one or more spaces. We can parse the same command using Python instead of awk.

Listing 6-3. Use Python to parse the process detail

```
>>> psout = 'oracle 1723  1  0 16:21 ? 00:00:01
/u01/app/oracle/product/12.1.0/dbhome_1/bin/tnslsnr LISTENER -inherit'
>>> type(psout)
<type 'str'>
>>> psoutlist = psout.split()
>>> type(psoutlist)
<type 'list'>
>>> psoutlist[7:]
['/u01/app/oracle/product/12.1.0/dbhome_1/bin/tnslsnr', 'LISTENER', '-inherit']
>>> ' '.join(psoutlist[7:])
'/u01/app/oracle/product/12.1.0/dbhome_1/bin/tnslsnr LISTENER -inherit'
>>> psoutstring = ' '.join(psoutlist[7:])
>>> psoutstring
'/u01/app/oracle/product/12.1.0/dbhome_1/bin/tnslsnr LISTENER -inherit'
```

psoutlist = psout.split() breaks apart the string into a list made up of string elements based on a delimiter of whitespace and assigns it to the psoutlist list object. psoutlist[7:] prints a subset of the psoutlist list object from the eighth (remember that a list index starts at 0) to the final element. psoutstring = ' '.join(psoutlist[7:]) joins the subset of elements back into a string delimited by a single space and assigns it to the psoutstring string object. What really makes Python shine is that this can all be done in one command, as shown in Listing 6-4.

Listing 6-4. Combine the commands from Listing 6-3 into a single command

```
>>> ' '.join('oracle 1723 1  0 16:21 ? 00:00:01
/u01/app/oracle/product/12.1.0/dbhome_1/bin/tnslsnr LISTENER -inherit'.split()[7:])
'/u01/app/oracle/product/12.1.0/dbhome_1/bin/tnslsnr LISTENER -inherit'
```

Listing 6-3 populates the psout variable directly with the output from the ps command. The process of capturing the output of the ps command could also be done directly from within Python, as shown in Listing 6-3a.

Listing 6-3a. Capture the **ps** command output using the Python subprocess module

```
>>> import subprocess
>>> mycommand = ['ps', '-ef']
>>> psoutput = subprocess.Popen(mycommand, stdout=subprocess.PIPE).communicate()[0].split('\n')
>>> for i in psoutput:
...     if 'tnslsnr' in i:
...         psout = i
```

Lists are a useful way of grouping strings and numbers together in Python, but sometimes a more complex object is required. Sometimes an index of single elements is not enough and we need a way of grouping keys and values together. This is especially true when working with EM CLI, where arrays are common and often complex. This is where Python dictionary objects come in.

Dictionaries

An equally important object type to understand in Python, and especially in EM CLI, is the "dictionary." Similar to Java's "hashtable," Perl's "hash" objects, and PL/SQL's "associative arrays," dictionaries are made up of a collection of key/value pairs. In other words, each element of the dictionary will be made up of one key and one value. The value can then be extracted by specifying its corresponding key. The syntax for calling a value is similar to that of calling a value in a list, but a key is specified instead of an index value. Listing 6-5 calls the value belonging to the key labeled 'second'.

Listing 6-5. Call a value from a dictionary by specifying the key to which it belongs

```
emcli>mydic = {'first': 'one', 'second': 'two', 'third': 'three', 'fourth': 'four', 'fifth': 'five'}
emcli>mydic['second']
'two'
```

Dictionaries use keys instead of a numerical index. JSON is represented as a dictionary object in Python since JSON is little more than an efficient key/value object. This can be shown clearly in EM CLI, as seen in Listing 6-6.

Listing 6-6. Use the **list( )** function in EM CLI to show a JSON dictionary

```
emcli>set_client_property('EMCLI_OUTPUT_TYPE', 'JSON')
emcli>list(resource='Targets').isJson()
True
emcli>type(list(resource='Targets').out())
<type 'dict'>
emcli>list(resource='Targets').out()
{'exceedsMaxRows': False, 'columnHeaders': ['TARGET_NAM...
```

Most EM CLI functions include an isJson function, which returns a boolean result indicating whether the result set will be JSON or not. This command indicates that the result set will return JSON instead of text.

By default, the interactive mode of EM CLI is text mode. The first command changes that behavior so that all result sets are returned as JSON.

The fourth line calls the out sub-function of the list function. This out function either prints to the screen or feeds to another object the output of the function that is calling it. In this case, the list function is returning information about the EM targets, and the type function is telling us that this output is being returned as a dictionary object.

The sixth line shows a very small part of the actual output, showing that it is contained within curly braces. The curly braces are what indicate that this object is a dictionary. Notice that one of the values is a list rather than a string. A dictionary value can be any other object type, including another dictionary.

Logon Script

It is necessary when using either interactive or scripting modes of EM CLI to establish a connection between EM CLI and the OMS. This is a repeatable procedure, so it is a good practice to have a script in place that can be called each time one calls a script or logs into EM CLI interactive mode.

The logon script is described below with comments regarding the various parts of it. The complete script is listed after the analysis.

The EM CLI classes and functions need to be imported first:

```
from emcli import *
```

This could also be done using a direct import:

```
import emcli
```

However, in this case each call to an EM CLI function would need to be qualified with the module name `emcli`. The next step is to identify an OMS in which to connect:

```
set_client_property('EMCLI_OMS_URL', 'https://em12cr3.example.com:7802/em')
```

Following that one needs either to identify a valid SSL certificate file by which to authenticate with the OMS or to specify that you trust any certificate presented:

```
set_client_property('EMCLI_CERT_LOC', '/path/to/cert.file')
```

or

```
set_client_property('EMCLI_TRUSTALL', 'true')
```

Optionally, you can specify which format you would like the commands to return: "JSON" or "TEXT." Unless there is a specific need for text output, JSON is the most versatile and easy to manipulate. However, it is also much more difficult to read:

```
set_client_property('EMCLI_OUTPUT_TYPE', 'JSON')
```

or

```
set_client_property('EMCLI_OUTPUT_TYPE', 'TEXT')
```

Finally, specify with which user you would like to log in and, optionally, that user's password. If the password is not specified, you will be prompted for it.:

```
print(login(username='sysman', password='foobar'))
```

The complete script is show in Listing 6-7.

Listing 6-7. **start.py** logon script

```
from emcli import *
set_client_property('EMCLI_OMS_URL', 'https://em12cr3.example.com:7802/em')
set_client_property('EMCLI_TRUSTALL', 'true')
set_client_property('EMCLI_OUTPUT_TYPE', 'JSON')
print(login(username='sysman', password='foobar'))
```

Although EM CLI may be started from the same directory that contains the logon script, Jython will not see it unless the directory is within its search path. Listing 6-8 shows the error message you would receive if the `start.py` file you are trying to import isn't in the Jython search path.

Listing 6-8. **start.py** not in the Jython search path

```
emcli>import start
Traceback (most recent call last):
  File "<stdin>", line 1, in <module>
ImportError: No module named start
```

The JYTHONPATH environment variable tells Jython the additional directories in which to search for modules to be imported. Set this variable before executing emcli. In Listing 6-9, the start module can now be successfully imported, either directly from the interactive mode command line or within a script in scripting mode.

Listing 6-9. Successful execution of the **start.py** script

```
[oracle@server ]$ export JYTHONPATH=/home/oracle/scripts
[oracle@server ]$ emcli
emcli>import start
Login successful
```

If you are not comfortable with including your password in the script (you shouldn't be) and only specify the username parameter with the login function, you will be prompted for the password:

```
Enter password : **********
```

Listing 6-10 shows an alternative method of authenticating that affords one the security of not including the password in the script while at the same time not requiring one to enter the password every time the script is invoked. The password in this example would be contained in the .secret file, which should have permissions set such that it can be read only by the operating system user invoking EM CLI.

Listing 6-10. **start.py** logon script using a password read from an external file

```
from emcli import *
set_client_property('EMCLI_OMS_URL', 'https://em12cr3.example.com:7802/em')
set_client_property('EMCLI_TRUSTALL', 'true')
set_client_property('EMCLI_OUTPUT_TYPE', 'JSON')
f = open('/home/oracle/.secret','r')
pwd = f.read()
print(login(username='sysman', password=pwd))
```

The steps included in the start.py script need to be executed every time EM CLI is invoked in scripted or interactive mode, which is why it is important to script the login process. Any script called directly should invoke the import start command before doing anything else.

Python Scripting with EM CLI to Set Target Properties

EM CLI includes a function to change the properties of a target. If the properties of a small number of targets need to be updated, it is easy to simply execute the set_target_property_value() function for each of those targets. When the need arises to update the properties of tens or even hundreds of targets, executing the function for each target is not efficient. Fortunately, with EM CLI we can take advantage of the full scripting functionality of Python.

A for loop can be used to iterate through any object and perform any task on each one of those object pieces. For example, it is common to add or update target properties after a target has been added. Any task involving changing target properties for more than a couple of targets in the GUI is tedious and time-consuming. There is more than one way to accomplish this task within EM CLI, but all of them are easier and more efficient than the GUI can offer.

For demonstration purposes, we'll use the interactive mode, but all of these commands will also work in scripting mode:

```
emcli>import start
Enter password :   *********
Login successful
```

Create an object containing all of the targets. Don't worry about filtering out targets yet. That part will be done further down in the script:

```
emcli>myobj = get_targets().out()['data']
emcli>len(myobj)
29
```

In this case, I know I have 29 targets in my repository. We want to update the Lifecycle Status and Location properties of the targets we just added that have the prefix of TEST_ with Development and COLO, respectively. Since we may want to add to or change this list of properties in the future, we'll put these into a dictionary as keys and values:

```
emcli>myprops = {'LifeCycle Status':'Development', 'Location':'COLO'}
```

We want to make sure we choose the correct targets for this update, so we will use regular expressions to filter the target names. Using regular expressions within Jython requires that we import another module:

```
emcli>import re
```

Now we can create the regular expression that we will use to filter the target names. This filter will be applied to each target name to determine if the target properties will be applied to that target:

```
emcli>filtermatch = '^TEST_'
emcli>myreg = re.compile(filtermatch)
```

Create a for loop to iterate through the targets. When writing programs like this, it is a good idea to write a little code and then test, especially when just getting started. Once the loop is created, we'll run it with a simple print command to make sure we are iterating through the appropriate information.

Make sure the lines shown in the example preceded by three dots are indented properly. An indentation in Python is four spaces:

```
emcli>for targ in myobj:
...    print(targ['Target Name'])
```

This shows us that we are able to see all of the target names in our repository. Now we can apply the filter so we are only seeing the targets that start with TEST_:

```
emcli>for targ in myobj:
...    if myreg.search(targ['Target Name']):
...        print(targ['Target Name'] + \
...                ' - ' + targ['Target Type'])
```

Now we are seeing just the targets we want to modify. Let's add in the command to change the properties. However, instead of running the commands blindly, we'll just print the command that the loop would have run to make sure the commands are what we want without actually affecting the targets:

```
emcli>for targ in myobj:
...     if myreg.search(targ['Target Name']):
...         mycommand = 'set_target_property_value(' + \
...                     'property_records="' + \
...                     targ['Target Name'] + ':' + \
...                     targ['Target Type'] + \
...                     ':LifeCycle Status:Development")'
...         print(mycommand)
set_target_property_value(property_records="TEST_em12cr3.example.com:host:LifeCycle
Status:Development")
set_target_property_value(property_records="TEST_em12cr3.example.com:3872:oracle_emd:LifeCycle
Status:Development")
```

The set_target_property_value() function commands are printed to the screen. These commands can then be copied and pasted within the same EM CLI session:

```
emcli>set_target_property_value(property_records="TEST_em12cr3.example.com:host:LifeCycle
Status:Development")
Properties updated successfully
```

However, a problem pops up immediately if we try to run the command for an agent target:

```
emcli>set_target_property_value(property_records="TEST_em12cr3.example.com:3872:oracle_emd:LifeCycle
Status:Development")
Syntax Error: Invalid value for parameter "INVALID_RECORD_ERR":
"em12cr3.example.com:3872:oracle_emd:LifeCycle Status:Development"
```

The target name TEST_em12cr3.example.com:3872 contains the default delimiter, the colon character, which means we need to include another parameter in the set_target_property_value() function to change the delimiter. The subseparator parameter will change the character that separates the different parts of the property_records parameter from a colon to an @ sign. Notice the addition of the mysubsep and myproprecs variables:

```
emcli>for targ in myobj:
...     if myreg.search(targ['Target Name']):
...         mysubsep = 'property_records=@'
...         myproprecs = targ['Target Name'] + \
...                      '@' + targ['Target Type'] + \
...                      '@LifeCycle Status@Development'
...         mycommand = 'set_target_property_value(' + \
...                     'subseparator="' + \
...                     mysubsep + '", property_records="' + \
...                     myproprecs + '")'
...         print(mycommand)
set_target_property_value(subseparator="property_records=@", property_records=" TEST_em12cr3.
                                example.com@host@LifeCycle Status@Development")
set_target_property_value(subseparator="property_records=@", property_records=" TEST_em12cr3.
                                example.com:3872@oracle_emd@LifeCycle Status@Development")
```

The commands are again printed to the screen. The properties for the TEST_em12cr3.example.com target have already been updated, so only the command to change the TEST_em12cr3.example.com:3872 target needs to be copied and pasted:

```
emcli>set_target_property_value(subseparator="property_records=@",
property_records="TEST_em12cr3.example.com:3872@oracle_emd@LifeCycle Status@Development")
Properties updated successfully
```

The example we just looked at hardcodes the properties. This will work fine if the properties never change, but at the beginning of this exercise we created the myprops dictionary so we could easily change the property keys and values:

```
emcli>myprops = {'LifeCycle Status':'Development', 'Location':'COLO'}
```

Now let's change the code we just created to take advantage of this variable. We'll continue to use the debugging mode we included in the code to print the commands to screen and then add a nested for loop inside the existing for loop; we'll then iterate through the items of the myprops dictionary. There is also an additional change here by adding the mydelim variable. By now you should be noticing a pattern; the more you parameterize, the easier your code is to read, change, troubleshoot, etc. Now if we decided to change the subseparator from an @ sign to something else, we would change it in one place, not four:

```
emcli>for targ in myobj:
...      if myreg.search(targ['Target Name']):
...          mydelim = '@'
...          mysubsep = 'property_records=' + mydelim
...          myproprecs = targ['Target Name'] + \
...                       mydelim + targ['Target Type'] + mydelim
...          for propkey, propvalue in myprops.items():
...              myproprecprops = propkey + mydelim + propvalue
...              mycommand = 'set_target_property_value(' + \
...                          'subseparator="' + \
...                          mysubsep + '", property_records="' + \
...                          myproprecs + \
...                          myproprecprops + '")'
...              print(mycommand)
```

These commands should work great for copy and paste, but we want to automate it further to skip the copy and paste and run the commands automatically in the code. However, when problems arise later, we don't want to lose the ability to look at this verbose output again, so we'll leave the debug in place and supplement it with the ability to choose whether we want to see the command printed to the screen or have it be run automatically by the script.

Adding a debug variable at the beginning of the script and checking for the value of that variable within the script is an easy way to enable or disable a "testing" mode. By default the debug variable will be false unless it is assigned a value, in which case it becomes true:

```
emcli>debug = ''
emcli>if debug:
...      print('True')
... else:
...      print('False')
...
False
```

```
emcli>debug = 'Yes'
emcli>if debug:
...      print('True')
... else:
...      print('False')
...
True
```

Now we can add this logic into the script and use it to decide whether we are debugging the script or executing it normally. There is also a line of output for normal execution mode that prints out some basic information about what the commands are doing:

```
emcli>debug = ''
emcli>for targ in myobj:
...      if myreg.search(targ['Target Name']):
...          mydelim = '@'
...          mysubsep = 'property_records=' + mydelim
...          myproprecs = targ['Target Name'] + mydelim + \
...                       targ['Target Type'] + mydelim
...          for propkey, propvalue in myprops.items():
...              myproprecprops = propkey + mydelim + propvalue
...              if debug:
...                  mycommand = 'set_target_property_value(' + \
...                              'subseparator="' + mysubsep + \
...                              '", property_records="' + \
...                              myproprecs + \
...                              myproprecprops + '")'
...                  print(mycommand)
...              else:
...                  print('Target: ' + targ['Target Name'] + \
...                        ' (' + targ['Target Type'] + \
...                        ')\n\tProperty: ' + propkey + \
...                        '\n\tValue:    ' + propvalue)
...                  set_target_property_value(
...                  subseparator=mysubsep,
...                  property_records=myproprecs + myproprecprops)
...
Target: TEST_em12cr3.example.com (host)
        Property: Location
        Value:    COLO
Properties updated successfully

Target: TEST_em12cr3.example.com (host)
        Property: LifeCycle Status
        Value:    Development
Properties updated successfully
```

This function makes things pretty easy, and we can easily change the properties or the target list filter. Using the debug variable, we can print out the commands instead of executing them. However, we can further simplify the process of updating target properties by moving all of these commands into a class. In addition, we'll add more functionality in order to make it more robust and less prone to errors.

Python Class with EM CLI to Set Target Properties

Creating a Python "class" allows us to "package" code into a single unit in which all of the code that is part of the class is both aware of and can use all of the other code within that class. From a class, one can create an "instance." An instance is an object in Python, and all of the changes to pieces of that instance are persistent for the life of that instance. Listing 6-11 shows the full text of the updateProps.py script, which contains the updateProps() class. For best results, create a file on the file system called updateProps.py and paste the full text of the code in it:

Listing 6-11. **update Props.py** creates the **updateProps( )** class

```python
import emcli
import re
import operator

class updateProps():
    def __init__(self, agentfilter='.*', typefilter='.*',
                 namefilter='.*', propdict={}):
        self.targs = []
        self.reloadtargs = True
        self.props(propdict)
        self.__loadtargobjects()
        self.filt(agentfilter=agentfilter, typefilter=typefilter,
                  namefilter=namefilter)
    def __loadtargobjects(self):
        if self.reloadtargs == True:
            self.reloadtargs = False
            self.fulltargs = \
              emcli.list(resource='Targets').out()['data']
            self.targprops = \
              emcli.list(resource='TargetProperties'
                         ).out()['data']
    def props(self, propdict):
        assert isinstance(propdict, dict), \
               'propdict parameter must be ' + \
               'a dictionary of ' + \
               '{"property_name":"property_value"}'
        self.propdict = propdict
    def filt(self, agentfilter='.*', typefilter='.*',
             namefilter='.*',
             sort=('TARGET_TYPE','TARGET_NAME'), show=False):
        self.targs = []
        __agentcompfilt = re.compile(agentfilter)
        __typecompfilt = re.compile(typefilter)
        __namecompfilt = re.compile(namefilter)
        self.__loadtargobjects()
        for __inttarg in self.fulltargs:
            if __typecompfilt.search(__inttarg['TARGET_TYPE']) \
               and __namecompfilt.search(
                   __inttarg['TARGET_NAME']) \
               and (__inttarg['EMD_URL'] == None or \
               __agentcompfilt.search(__inttarg['EMD_URL'])):
                 self.targs.append(__inttarg)
        __myoperator = operator
```

```python
        for __myop in sort:
            __myoperator = operator.itemgetter(__myop)
        self.targssort = sorted(self.targs, key=__myoperator)
        if show == True:
            self.show()
    def show(self):
        print('%-5s%-40s%s' % (
            ' ', 'TARGET_TYPE'.ljust(40, '.'),
            'TARGET_NAME'))
        print('%-15s%-30s%s\n%s\n' % (
            ' ', 'PROPERTY_NAME'.ljust(30, '.'),
            'PROPERTY_VALUE', '=' * 80))
        for __inttarg in self.targssort:
            print('%-5s%-40s%s' % (
                ' ', __inttarg['TARGET_TYPE'].ljust(40, '.'),
                __inttarg['TARGET_NAME']))
            self.__showprops(__inttarg['TARGET_GUID'])
            print('')
    def __showprops(self, guid):
        self.__loadtargobjects()
        for __inttargprops in self.targprops:
            __intpropname = \
                __inttargprops['PROPERTY_NAME'].split('_')
            if __inttargprops['TARGET_GUID'] == guid and \
                __intpropname[0:2] == ['orcl', 'gtp']:
                print('%-15s%-30s%s' %
                    (' ', ' '.join(__intpropname[2:]).ljust(
                        30, '.'),
                        __inttargprops['PROPERTY_VALUE']))
    def setprops(self, show=False):
        assert len(self.propdict) > 0, \
            'The propdict parameter must contain ' + \
            'at least one property. Use the ' + \
            'props() function to modify.'
        self.reloadtargs = True
        __delim = '@#&@#&&'
        __subseparator = 'property_records=' + __delim
        for __inttarg in self.targs:
            for __propkey, __propvalue \
                in self.propdict.items():
                __property_records = __inttarg['TARGET_NAME'] + \
                    __delim + __inttarg['TARGET_TYPE'] + \
                    __delim + __propkey + __delim + __propvalue
                print('Target: ' + __inttarg['TARGET_NAME'] +
                    ' (' + __inttarg['TARGET_TYPE'] +
                    ')\n\tProperty: '
                    + __propkey + '\n\tValue: ' +
                    __propvalue + '\n')
                emcli.set_target_property_value(
                    subseparator=__subseparator,
                    property_records=__property_records)
        if show == True:
            self.show()
```

Once there is a file containing the code, we can use this code to update the properties of Enterprise Manager targets. Start a session of EM CLI and establish a login to the OMS.

Using the updateProps( ) Class

Listing 6-12 shows an example of how to use the updateProps() class to update the properties of some EM CLI targets. The class is doing exactly what the commands did in the previous section, but you will notice how much less code is required.

Listing 6-12. Import and use the **updateProps( )** class to change target properties

```
emcli>import updateProps
emcli>myinst = updateProps.updateProps()
emcli>myinst.props({'LifeCycle Status':'Development'})
emcli>myinst.filt(namefilter='^em12cr3.example.com$', typefilter='host')
emcli>myinst.show()
      TARGET_TYPE...........................TARGET_NAME
                 PROPERTY_NAME.................PROPERTY_VALUE
===============================================================================

      host..................................em12cr3.example.com
                 target version...............6.4.0.0.0
                 os...........................Linux
                 platform.....................x86_64

emcli>myinst.setprops(show=True)
Target: em12cr3.example.com (host)
      Property: LifeCycle Status
      Value: Development

      TARGET_TYPE...........................TARGET_NAME
                 PROPERTY_NAME.................PROPERTY_VALUE
===============================================================================

      host..................................em12cr3.example.com
                 target version...............6.4.0.0.0
                 os...........................Linux
                 platform.....................x86_64
                 lifecycle status............Development
```

The example in Listing 6-12 updated one property for one target. The updateProps() class is capable of updating any number of properties for any number of targets. Listing 6-13 expands on the previous example by updating additional properties of the same target.

Listing 6-13. Expand the properties to be updated

```
emcli>myinst.props({'LifeCycle Status':'Development', 'Location':'COLO', 'Comment':'Test EM'})
emcli>myinst.setprops(show=True)
Target: em12cr3.example.com (host)
        Property: Location
        Value: COLO

Target: em12cr3.example.com (host)
        Property: LifeCycle Status
        Value: Development

Target: em12cr3.example.com (host)
        Property: Comment
        Value: Test EM

    TARGET_TYPE...........................TARGET_NAME
            PROPERTY_NAME.................PROPERTY_VALUE
==============================================================================

    host..................................em12cr3.example.com
            target version...............6.4.0.0.0
            os...........................Linux
            platform.....................x86_64
            location.....................COLO
            comment......................Test EM
            lifecycle status.............Development
```

We did not change the target filter. The only things we changed about the `myinst` instance were the properties to be updated. The `myinst.props()` function changed the properties to be applied to the targets. The output showed that three different properties for the same target were updated.

Let's assume that we want the same three properties applied to additional targets but the only targets we want them applied to are the host and agent targets of the Enterprise Manager OMS server. We will leave the properties alone, but we'll update the target filter to include the additional target type of `oracle_emd`, as shown in Listing 6-14.

Listing 6-14. Change the target type to include the agent target

```
emcli>myinst.filt(namefilter='^em12cr3.example.com.*$', typefilter='host|oracle_emd')
emcli>myinst.show()
    TARGET_TYPE...........................TARGET_NAME
            PROPERTY_NAME.................PROPERTY_VALUE
==============================================================================

    host..................................em12cr3.example.com
            target version...............6.4.0.0.0
            os...........................Linux
            platform.....................x86_64
            location.....................COLO
            comment......................Test EM
            lifecycle status.............Development
```

```
        oracle_emd.............................em12cr3.example.com:3872
                os.............................Linux
                platform.......................x86_64
                target version.................12.1.0.3.0
emcli>myinst.setprops(show=True)
Target: em12cr3.example.com (host)
        Property: Location
        Value: COLO

Target: em12cr3.example.com (host)
        Property: LifeCycle Status
        Value: Development

Target: em12cr3.example.com (host)
        Property: Comment
        Value: Test EM

Target: em12cr3.example.com:3872 (oracle_emd)
        Property: Location
        Value: COLO

Target: em12cr3.example.com:3872 (oracle_emd)
        Property: LifeCycle Status
        Value: Development

Target: em12cr3.example.com:3872 (oracle_emd)
        Property: Comment
        Value: Test EM

    TARGET_TYPE..............................TARGET_NAME
                PROPERTY_NAME..................PROPERTY_VALUE
================================================================================

        host..................................em12cr3.example.com
                target version................6.4.0.0.0
                os............................Linux
                platform......................x86_64
                location......................COLO
                comment.......................Test EM
                lifecycle status..............Development

        oracle_emd............................em12cr3.example.com:3872
                os............................Linux
                platform......................x86_64
                lifecycle status..............Development
                location......................COLO
                comment.......................Test EM
                target version................12.1.0.3.0
```

The functionality of the updateProps() is extensive and can be as granular or as broad as you would like. A more detailed description of how to use it can be found in Chapter 8. The best way to fully exploit the updateProps() class is to understand the code itself.

Understanding the Code

Now that we've seen the code itself as well as an overview of how it works, we'll analyze the code to understand what is going on behind the scenes. Understanding the code will not only help you exploit all of its functionality, it will also allow you to customize it to your tastes and needs.

The first thing to notice is that everything after the class declaration is indented by at least four spaces. This means that all of the code after the class declaration is part of the class. Within the class are function declarations, and beneath each function is the code that belongs to that function. Let's break this down into smaller pieces so as to understand what exactly the code is doing and why using a class offers significant advantages.

The first function shown in Listing 6-15 is called __init__(). This is a reserved function name that will automatically be executed when the class is called. The word self is a reference to the instance created from the class. When an instance variable or object (preceded by self.) is created, it is a variable or object assigned to the instance for the life of that instance. When the myinst instance is created from updateProps(), the list object targs and boolean variable reloadtargs are created as well. Instance variables and objects can be viewed as part of the instance in most cases.

Listing 6-15. __init__() is the initial function of the **updateProps()** class

```
def __init__(self, agentfilter='.*', typefilter='.*',
            namefilter='.*', propdict={}):
    self.targs = []
    self.reloadtargs = True
    self.props(propdict)
    self.__loadtargobjects()
    self.filt(agentfilter=agentfilter, typefilter=typefilter,
            namefilter=namefilter)
```

In Listing 6-16, we create an instance object of the updateProps() class by creating an instance of (executing) the class and assigning that execution to a variable. Then we can print out the reloadtargs instance variable. Notice that the word without parentheses is a class and the same word *with* parentheses is an instance.

Listing 6-16. Create an instance from the class

```
emcli>import updateProps
emcli>myinst = updateProps.updateProps()
emcli>print(myinst.reloadtargs)
False
emcli>type(updateProps.updateProps)
<type 'classobj'>
emcli>type(updateProps.updateProps())
<type 'instance'>
emcli>type(myinst)
<type 'instance'>
```

The last four lines of the __init__ function call the props, __loadtargobjects, and filt functions. The props function, which sets the property keys and values, the __loadtargobjects function, which caches the target information, and the filt function, which allows us to filter the targets assigned to the instance, are defined further down in the class. Creating an instance parses the entire class before processing commands, so the ordering of functions within a class is not important.

The querying of the target information is a fairly expensive process and can take between one and twenty seconds to run. The __loadtargobjects function, as shown in Listing 6-17, is a performance-tuning function that makes the execution of the class more efficient. It only queries and loads the target information on the creation of the instance by being called within the __init__ function, and then only when self.reloadtargs is set to true.

Listing 6-17. The **__loadtargobjects( )** of the **updateProps( )** class reloads the EM targets when necessary

```python
def __loadtargobjects(self):
    if self.reloadtargs == True:
        self.reloadtargs = False
        self.fulltargs = \
          emcli.list(resource='Targets').out()['data']
        self.targprops = \
          emcli.list(resource='TargetProperties'
                      ).out()['data']
```

The props( ) function shown in Listing 6-18 sets or modifies the propsdict variable, which holds the key value dictionary that is used to set the target properties. This was turned into a function rather than just setting the parameter directly, mainly because it can be called multiple times and includes the assert statement for error checking.

Listing 6-18. The **props( )** function of the **updateProps( )** class updates the **propsdict** properties dictionary

```python
def props(self, propdict):
    assert isinstance(propdict, dict), \
            'propdict parameter must be ' + \
            'a dictionary of ' + \
            '{"property_name":"property_value"}'
    self.propdict = propdict
```

Listing 6-19 shows the filt( ) function, which defines the scope of targets to which the defined properties will be applied for this instance. Even after the filter is applied, it can be queried or changed. The first three parameters (agentfilter, typefilter, and namefilter) are compiled as regular expressions so as to include or exclude targets for this instance. If the parameters are not defined when the filt( ) function is called, they are defined implicitly to include all targets. The sort parameter defines how the filtered targets should be sorted, and, finally, the show parameter determines if the output of the filtered target list will be printed to screen.

Listing 6-19. The **filt( )** function of the **updateProps( )** class creates and manages the filtered list of targets

```python
def filt(self, agentfilter='.*', typefilter='.*',
        namefilter='.*',
        sort=('TARGET_TYPE','TARGET_NAME'), show=False):
    self.targs = []
    __agentcompfilt = re.compile(agentfilter)
    __typecompfilt = re.compile(typefilter)
    __namecompfilt = re.compile(namefilter)
    self.__loadtargobjects()
    for __inttarg in self.fulltargs:
        if __typecompfilt.search(__inttarg['TARGET_TYPE']) \
            and __namecompfilt.search(
                __inttarg['TARGET_NAME']) \
            and (__inttarg['EMD_URL'] == None or \
            __agentcompfilt.search(__inttarg['EMD_URL'])):
            self.targs.append(__inttarg)
    __myoperator = operator
    for __myop in sort:
        __myoperator = operator.itemgetter(__myop)
    self.targssort = sorted(self.targs, key=__myoperator)
    if show == True:
        self.show()
```

`self.targs = []` defines or clears a list to store the filtered targets. The next three lines compile the regular expressions for the first three filter parameters. `self.__loadtargobjects()` calls the `__loadtargobjects()` function to reload the full target list. The `for __inttarg in self.fulltargs:` loop and its nested `if` statement create the filtered target list based on the filter parameters. The `__myoperator =` operator and the following three lines define the sort key and sort the filtered target list. Finally, the filtered, sorted list can be printed to screen.

Unless the target properties defined for the myinst instance should be applied to all of the targets, the `filt` function needs to be called. When the instance is created, the target list is created as well and includes every target defined in Enterprise Manager. The `targs` instance list object shows the number of targets currently defined for the instance, as shown in Listing 6-20.

Listing 6-20. *When an instance of* **updateProps( )** *is created, it includes all targets*

```
emcli>len(myinst.targs)
29
```

If this instance filtered list is modified, the length of the `targs` object will reflect the change, as shown in Listing 6-21.

Listing 6-21. *The instance targets are pared down with the* **filt( )** *function*

```
emcli>myinst.filt(namefilter='^orcl.*\.example\.com')
emcli>len(myinst.targs)
2
```

The filtering of the target list could also take place during instance creation, as shown in Listing 6-22.

Listing 6-22. *The instance targets are pared down as part of the instance creation*

```
emcli>myinst = updateProps.updateProps(namefilter='^orcl.*\.example\.com')
emcli>len(myinst.targs)
2
```

We probably wouldn't want to make target property changes without first knowing the target names and the currently defined properties for those targets. The `show()` function in Listing 6-23 allows us to see this information, printed in a format that is easier to read than JSON or a Python dictionary.

Listing 6-23. *The* **show( )** *function of the* **updateProps( )** *class previews the instance target list along with their currently allocated properties*

```
def show(self):
    print('%-5s%-40s%s' % (
            ' ', 'TARGET_TYPE'.ljust(40, '.'),
            'TARGET_NAME'))
    print('%-15s%-30s%s\n%s\n' % (
            ' ', 'PROPERTY_NAME'.ljust(30, '.'),
            'PROPERTY_VALUE', '=' * 80))
    for __inttarg in self.targssort:
        print('%-5s%-40s%s' % (
                ' ', __inttarg['TARGET_TYPE'].ljust(40, '.'),
                __inttarg['TARGET_NAME']))
        self.__showprops(__inttarg['TARGET_GUID'])
        print('')
```

The __showprops() function shown in Listing 6-24 is called from the show() function in a recursive manner to retrieve each target property defined for a target. In other words, the __showprops() function is called once for each target defined for the instance, and the properties defined for the target are stored with it as child records.

Listing 6-24. The __**showprops( )** function of the **updateProps( )** class is called to retrieve the properties for each target defined in the instance

```
def __showprops(self, guid):
    self.__loadtargobjects()
    for __inttargprops in self.targprops:
        __intpropname = \
            __inttargprops['PROPERTY_NAME'].split('_')
        if __inttargprops['TARGET_GUID'] == guid and \
            __intpropname[0:2] == ['orcl', 'gtp']:
            print('%-15s%-30s%s' %
                    (' ', ' '.join(__intpropname[2:]).ljust(
                    30, '.'),
                    __inttargprops['PROPERTY_VALUE']))
```

Finally, Listing 6-25 shows the setprops() function, which is called to make the magic happen. At the point that this function is called, the filtered target list has already been defined and the propdict dictionary variable is populated with the property name–value pairs that will be set for the filtered target list.

Listing 6-25. The __**setprops( )** function of the **updateProps( )** class is called to apply the properties updates

```
def setprops(self, show=False):
    assert len(self.propdict) > 0, \
            'The propdict parameter must contain ' + \
            'at least one property. Use the ' + \
            'props() function to modify.'
    self.reloadtargs = True
    __delim = '@#&@#&&'
    __subseparator = 'property_records=' + __delim
    for __inttarg in self.targs:
        for __propkey, __propvalue \
            in self.propdict.items():
            __property_records = __inttarg['TARGET_NAME'] + \
                __delim + __inttarg['TARGET_TYPE'] + \
                __delim + __propkey + __delim + __propvalue
            print('Target: ' + __inttarg['TARGET_NAME'] +
                    ' (' + __inttarg['TARGET_TYPE'] +
                    ')\n\tProperty: '
                    + __propkey + '\n\tValue: ' +
                    __propvalue + '\n')
            emcli.set_target_property_value(
                subseparator=__subseparator,
                property_records=__property_records)
    if show == True:
        self.show()
```

The `assert` statement does some error checking to make sure that there is at least one property name–value pair in the `propdict` variable to set on the target list. `self.reloadtargs = True` tells the instance that the target and properties information should be freshly queried from the database after the new target properties have been set. `__delim = '@#&@#&&'` is a set of characters that should never be found in a target or property name and is used as the delimiter in the `emcli.set_target_property_value()` function. `__subseparator = 'property_records=' + __delim` is also used for formatting.

The first `for` loop iterates through the filtered target list. The second `for` loop iterates through the `propdict` variable. Inside the second nested for loop is the `emcli.set_target_property_value()` function, which actually sets the properties on each target. This set_target_property_value() function is executed once for each property per target, so the total number of executions of this function will be the number of records in the filtered target list multiplied by the number of property name–value pairs in `propdict`. As each property is set, a result is printed to the screen.

Using a class in Python requires a little extra time and effort up front, but it is well worth it. The code you work so hard to create is scalable, extensible, and reusable. You can reuse code from any classes you create and do not have to worry about testing them again.

Summary

Enterprise Manager is truly a powerful tool. Having a firm grasp of the functions of the graphical interface are essential to using it effectively. EM CLI greatly enhances the ability to take advantage of all of the powerful features of EM. EM CLI isn't the easiest thing to learn, but having the ability to script and automate activities through it offers a clear advantage for the administrator.

Python is a powerful programming language whose maturity has been tested over the last 20-plus years. EM CLI is written in Jython, the Java implementation of Python. Jython allows the administrator to increase their EM effectiveness by taking advantage of the power and agility of Python alongside EM CLI.

The learning curve of any command-line tool is high, but the Python language and EM CLI are quite intuitive. If you get stuck on syntax or functionality, help is plentiful and easy to come by. This chapter gives examples that were created out of necessity in real-world production environments where it wasn't feasible to do these tasks through the GUI.

The real-world environments you, the reader, will face may differ from those here, but the principals and much of the code demonstrated in this chapter can be used to create effective and efficient solutions for the Enterprise administrator.

■ ■ ■

## CHAPTER 7

Using the Software Library and Oracle Extensibility Exchange

The OEM Software Library

Creating a software library ensures that all provisioning, patching, and scripting entities are stored in a location available to the OEM repository; this conserves resources and costs for the IT infrastructure. The concept appears simple enough, but often you enter an IT organization and find that there are multiple sources for installation media, patch locations, and so on. Having a central software library that is configured within the EM12c environment and sized appropriately (100 GB minimum for small environments, 250 GB minimum for extensive and HA/MAA [High Availability/Maximum Availability Architecture] environments) ensures that provisioning, patching, and scripting can be supported for the life of the OEM system.

The added benefit to a central library for software is the reduction of repeating tasks, such as downloading software or recreating valuable scripts, deployment procedures, and other Enterprise Manager entities.

Software Library

EM12c offers a valuable feature: the OEM software library. The shared storage location must be configured before you're able to utilize and administer the software library. This requires a repository that can be referenced and is located in shared file storage, either an OMS shared file system or an OMS agent file location on the host where the OMS resides.

When planning the design of the software library storage, consider the OMS environment design. If multiple OMS instances exist, then a shared or mounted path would be the best option. Depending on the decision, the configuration will be slightly different for the software library storage setup.

Setting Up Software Library Storage

There are two paths by which this can be achieved, either from the Setup menu for Provisioning and Patching or from the left option, Cloud Control. The interface shown in Figure 7-1 can be accessed in the EM12c console without the Cloud Control plugin by clicking on Setup, Provisioning and Patching, then on Software Library.

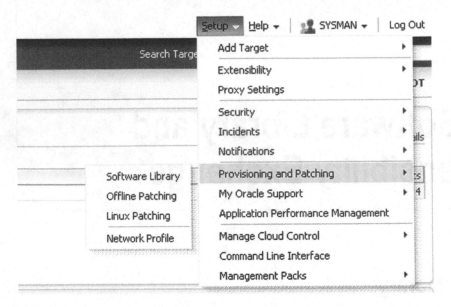

Figure 7-1. *The Setup menu dropdown to access the software library*

Once in this wizard, you have the option to view either OMS shared file systems or OMS agent file systems. As of 12.1.0.3, Oracle recommends that if scripts are to be shared among agent hosts the latter is preferable, but for our example in Figure 7-1, we are going to use an OMS shared file system for the script repository.

Ensure that any location chosen to become a software library storage location has enough space to retain all current and future entities, including future patches and installations to ease management challenges. Minimum guidelines for sizing the software library were offered earlier in this chapter; keep these in mind as you choose the location so that a secondary repository isn't required later on.

You can add as many file locations and referenced file locations as required for your OMS configuration (Figure 7-2). Referenced file locations refer to files located on agent hosts and are a read-only location via the software library.

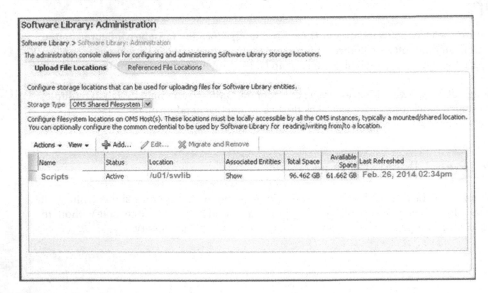

Figure 7-2. *The EM12c software library interface, displaying an existing OMS shared file system*

For multiple OMS environments, you should configure the software library in a non-local shared file system so it will be accessible to any of the OMS environments.

For the OMS agent file system, the agent simply requires access to the OMS host. This configuration requires a named or preferred credential setup prior to setup of the agent file system to ensure success. There is an option to create the preferred credential at the time of the OMS agent file system setup, but failure has been reported in some Release 2 versions. For this reason, I recommend having the preferred credentials configured before attempting the agent file system setup.

Once you have clicked the Add button in the software library configuration interface, the screen in Figure 7-3 will appear:

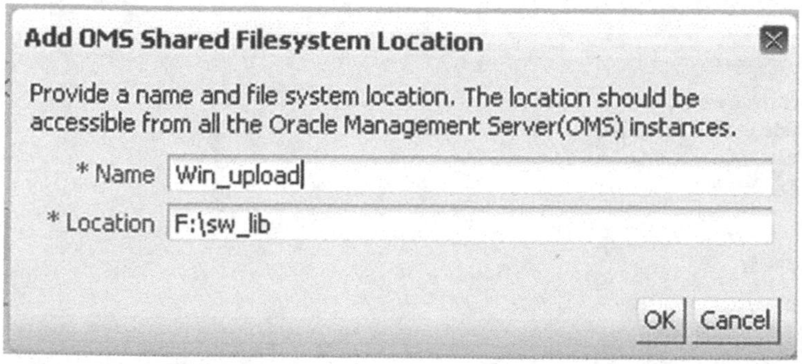

Figure 7-3. *Creating a shared file system to be used with the software library*

An alias can be provided for any OMS file system for the location, and then the path for the shared file system is entered. Figure 7-3 shows a Windows OMS host; the path is showing a drive letter assignment as opposed to a volume entry that we would use on a Unix/Linux environment. Once satisfied with the information provided, the administrator clicks OK and the shared file system is created.

To create a new software library location with the EM CLI, you can perform the following:

```
emcli add_swlib_storage_location
        -name="WIN_UPLOAD"
        -path="F:\sw_lib "
```

This will create a new OMS shared file system that can be used just the same as any created from the console. An agent shared file system can be created via the EM CLI with the following command:

```
emcli add_swlib_storage_location
        -name="Agent_WIN_UPLOAD"
        -path="F:\swlib"
        -type="OmsAgent"
        -host="orcl.us.acme.com"
        -credential_name="MyOrclCreds"
        -credential_owner="ORCL_USER"
```

This shared agent file system is now ready and will utilize existing credentials set up in the EM12c environment as well as use a shared volume directory path of /u01/swlib.

The third option is a referenced file location. This is used only if the file is stored outside the software library and will be deployed from this referenced location.

Checking In Entities

Best practice recommends creating a standalone folder within the Enterprise Manager software library to house scripts or other miscellaneous entities. This is a simple task when performed from the EM12c console.

From the console, click on Enterprise, Provisioning and Patching, and then Software Library, as shown in Figure 7-4.

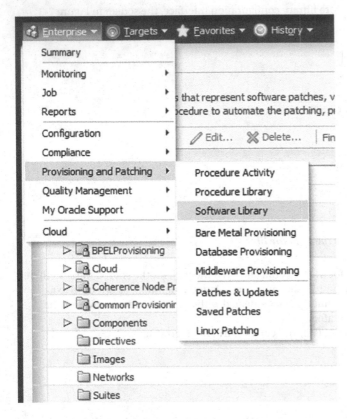

Figure 7-4. *Accessing the software library in EM12c*

In the software library, a number of folders are already present, but a new one should be created to house scripts. Right click on Software Library (the top tier in the directory) and click on Create Folder (Figure 7-5).

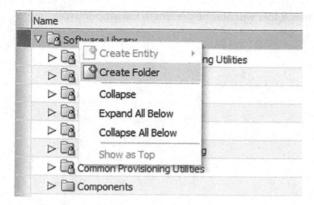

Figure 7-5. *Creating a folder in the EM12c software library*

The screen in Figure 7-6 comes up and allows you to enter information pertaining to the folder.

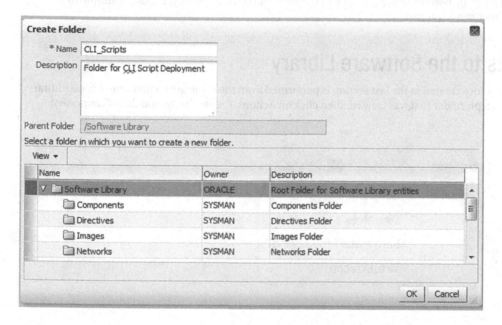

Figure 7-6. *Information entries about a folder to be created in the software library*

Enter a name that clearly defines the use for the folder and add a description that will assist anyone who reads the folder's properties. Verify that you want to create the folder in the parent directory of the software library and, once satisfied, click OK.

Returning to the main page of the software library, the new folder will now be present in the dropdown (Figure 7-7):

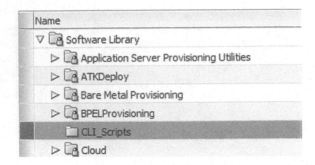

Figure 7-7. *The new folder just created for command-line scripts in the software library*

This is the folder that will be used to house the EM CLI scripts in the software library, making it simple to distinguish them from other stored entities.

Adding Scripts to the Software Library

Loading scripts from the folder created in the last section is performed from the same area within the software library. First, highlight the CLI_Scripts folder that was created, then click on Actions, Create Entity, and then Component (Figure 7-8).

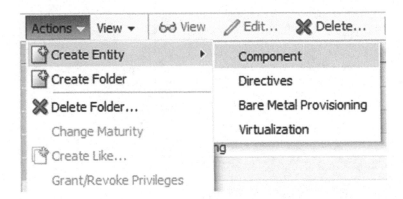

Figure 7-8. *Adding scripting to the software library, a.k.a., creating entities*

The script is going to be built out as a single component that can be deployed from the software library. Multiple scripts can be stored within one component if they are part of a single deployment process.

You have the choice to upload files into the library or to refer to files (a reference). For the example here, the goal is to check in a script. It will be stored as a single, generic component (a.k.a. entity).

Choose the software library location that will be uploaded to. In our example, we will use the default shared location for uploading. The logical location will be our CLI_Scripts folder within the console.

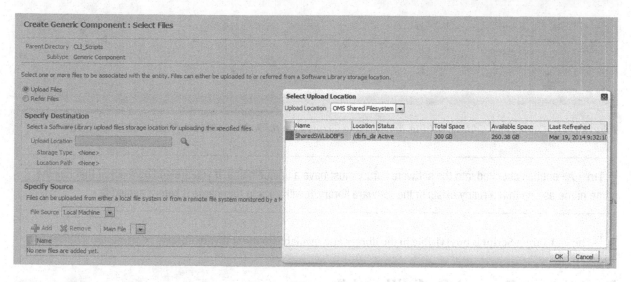

Figure 7-9. *How to create generic components and select files in the software library*

Click on OK and you'll be prompted with a second window where you can provide information about the entity (i.e., script) you are about to add to the software library (Figure 7-10).

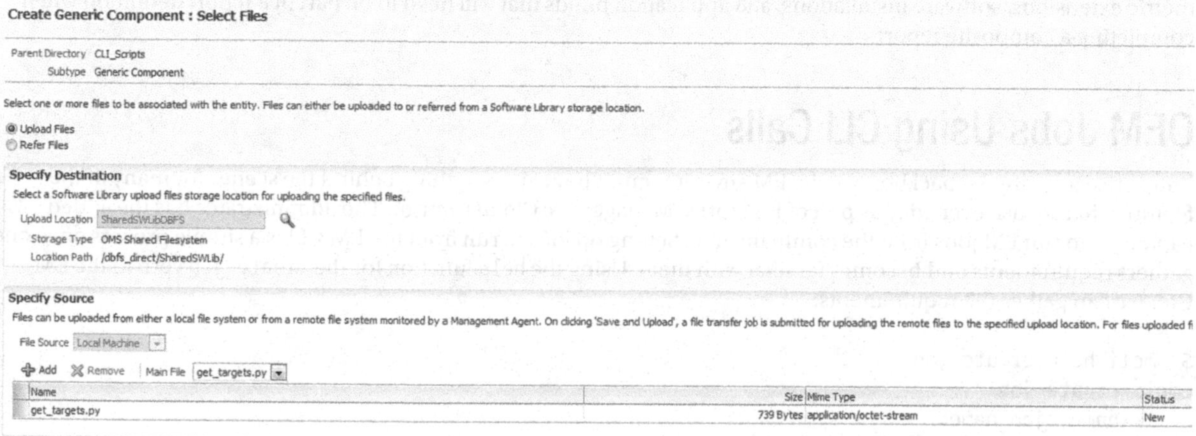

Figure 7-10. *Entering descriptive data and path information about scripts to be uploaded to the software library*

Click on Next to add the script. The script we are uploading is a simple one that lists out targets in an aesthetically appealing view (Figure 7-11). Click on the Add button, browse to the script (it can be local on the workstation), and click OK. Click Save, as we don't need to add any other provisioning information, and the upload of the script to the software library is complete.

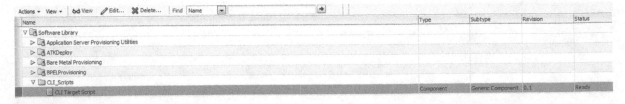

Figure 7-11. *Options for adding, editing, and deleting scripts from the software library folder CLI Target Script*

■ **Tip** All entities checked into the software library must have a unique name. If you are adding a script that has the same name as one that already exists in the software library, it will ask you to rename it before adding it.

The CLI Target Script is now visible in the library and available to the software library.

Building a Report Definition Library

The software library folders can be built out to then create a library available to the repository, rather than writing new scripts each time or having scripts housed on different hosts or workstations.

Plan out the library carefully, just as you did for the other entities. Create a separate library folder location and consider the space allocation required for this type of provisioning. Plan for entities from other features, such as metric extensions, software installations, and application builds that will need to be part of a report definition when completing a composite report.

OEM Jobs Using CLI Calls

Enterprise jobs are the backbone of the EM environment. They run everything behind the scenes for many of the features that we use every day as part of Enterprise Manager 12c Cloud Control. The administrator has the added capability to run EM jobs from the command line. Setting up jobs to run from the EM CLI is a simple process once one gathers requirements and becomes familiar with them. Using the help function for the create_job verb in the EM CLI, we can gather the requirements:

```
$ emcli help create_job
emcli create_job
    -name=<job_name>
    -type=<job_type>
    -input_file="property_file:<filename>"
Description:
 Create and schedule a job.

Options:
    -name: Optional parameter. The name may be specified in the input file instead.
    -type: Optional parameter. The type may be specified in the input file instead.
    -input_file: Required parameter. <filename> must be provided to load the properties for
                 creating and scheduling the job.
```

A template property file for the job_type can be obtained using EMCLI verb "describe_job_type".
Another job of the same job type could also be used to generate the property file using EMCLI verb
"describe_job".
Please make sure that the property file is accessible to the EMCLI client for reading.

Sample:
Create and schedule a job with name MYJOB1 and of job type MyJobType1 with property file present at
location /tmp/myjob1_prop.txt
    emcli create_job -name=MYJOB1 -job_type=MyJobType1 -
input_file="property_file:/tmp/myjob1_prop.txt"

Create a Job

The following steps must be performed to create a job. In our example, we will first perform upgrades to six existing
agents' hosts and then remove those previous agents.

To upgrade:

1. Check to see what agents are available for upgrades.

2. Input and use file to list those agents and use said file as part of our job.

3. Upgrade the agents.

4. Check the status of the process once upgrade is completed.

To remove previous agents:

1. Check on what existing agents' installations can be cleaned up after the upgrade.

2. Use EM CLI to uninstall the old agent installation.

3. Use an EM CLI host command to remove each of the old agent home directories.

Step 1: Upgrade Agents

List out the agents that we'll be upgrading as part of the EM job:

```
>emcli get_upgradable_agents > /u01/app/scripts/upg_agents.txt

orcl2:3872 12.1.0.2.0 12.1.0.3.0 Linux x86-64
 /u01/app/oracle/Agent12c/core/12.1.0.2.0
orcl1:3872 12.1.0.2.0 12.1.0.3.0 Linux x86-64 /u01/app/oracle/Agent12c/core/12.1.0.2.0

>vi /u01/app/scripts/upg_agents.txt
```
Remove the version information and the platform. You should be left with is the agent host and port:
```
orcl2:3872
orcl1:3872
...
```

Use this file to create an EM job that upgrades the agents and ensures the stage_location direction value has at least 2 GB of space:

```
>emcli upgrade_agents -input_file="agents_file:/u01/app/scripts/upg_agents.txt" -job_
name="UPG_021814_AGENTS" -stage_location=/u01/app/jobs
The agent list size is 6
```

Upgradable Agents

```
Agent Installed Version Version After Upgrade Platform Oracle Home
----- ---------------- --------------------- -------- ----
orcl2:3872 12.1.0.2.0 12.1.0.3.0 Linux x86-64 /u01/app/oracle/agent12c/core/12.1.0.2.0
orcl1:3872 12.1.0.2.0 12.1.0.3.0 Linux x86-64 /u01/app/oracle/agent12c/core/12.1.0.2.0
```

You can run the the root.sh from the EM CLI to each of the hosts that have been granted root/sudo privileges (one more reason to be offered this access via the EM12c environment). If the preferred credentials do NOT have root access, then you will need to run it manually via the EM CLI or from each of the agent targets to complete the installations.

```
Agent Reason
----- ------
orcl1:3872 Preferred Privileged Credential for Oracle Home of Agent : Not Set | Privilege Delegation
for Host : Not Set
```

Once the agent has been upgraded, you will see the following message so you can check the status of the job quickly from within the console:

```
Agent Upgrade Job submitted for Upgradable Agents shown above. Use emcli get_agent_upgrade_status
command or goto EM CONSOLE -> Set Up -> Manage Cloud Control -> Upgrade Agents -> Agent Upgrade
Results to see job status
Job Name : UPG_021814_AGENTS
>emcli get_agent_upgrade_status -job_name=UPG_021814_AGENTS
```

```
Showing for each agent in the job UPG_021814_AGENTS
```

```
Agent Status Started Ended
----- ------ ------- -----
orcl2:3872 Running 2014-02-18 15:32:58 MST -
orcl1:3872 Running 2014-02-18 15:32:58 MST -
...
```

If any failures occurred, you will want to check those via the console for the easiest access, or you will need to query the EM repository. For this example, we will look at the high-level status:

```
>emcli get_agent_upgrade_status -job_name=UPG_021814_AGENTS
```

```
Showing for each agent in the job UPG_021814_AGENTS
```

```
Agent Status Started Ended
----- ------ ------- -----
orcl2:3872 Success 2014-02-18 15:32:08 MST 2014-02-18 15:53:22 MST
...
```

We can now use this information to create the input file for the next step of removing all of the agents' installations we no longer want in our EM12c environment:

```
>emcli get_signoff_agents -output_file="/u01/app/work/signoff_021814.txt"
```

The previous command will send to an output file that can be used for the next step:

```
Agents available for Sign-off

Agent Installed Version Platform Oracle Home

----- ----------------- -------- -----------

orcl2:3872 12.1.0.3.0 Linux x86-64 /u01/app/oracle/agent12c/core/12.1.0.3.0

orcl1:3872 12.1.0.3.0 Linux x86-64 /u02/oracle/agent12cR2/core/12.1.0.3.0

orcl3:3872 12.1.0.3.0 Linux x86-64 /u01/app/oracle/agent12c/core/12.1.0.3.0

orcl4:3872 12.1.0.3.0 Linux x86-64 /u01/app/oracle/agent12c/core/12.1.0.3.0

emrp2:3872 12.1.0.3.0 Linux x86-64 /u01/app/oracle/agent12c/core/12.1.0.3.0

orcl6:3872 12.1.0.3.0 Linux x86-64 /u01/app/oracle/agent12c/core/12.1.0.3.0
```

To view output of file:

```
>cat /u01/app/oracle/work/signoff_agents.txt

orcl2:3872
orcl1:3872
orcl3:3872
orcl4:3872
emrp2:3872
orcl6:3872
```

Step 2: Remove Old Agents

Our second example will clean up agents now that we've upgraded all of them. Remove agents by using a match string in the search via an EM CLI signoff_agents command:

```
>emcli signoff_agents -agents="oradba%" -job_name=CLEANUP_12cR2_AGNTS

Agents available for Sign-off

Agent Installed Version Platform Oracle Home

----- ----------------- -------- -----------
```

```
orcl2:3872 12.1.0.3.0 Linux x86-64 /u01/app/oracle/agent12c/core/12.1.0.3.0

orcl1:3872 12.1.0.3.0 Linux x86-64 /u01/app/oracle/agent12c/core/12.1.0.3.0

Agent Sign-off Job Submitted for the above agents. Use emcli get_signoff_status or goto EM CONSOLE
-> Set Up -> Manage Cloud Control -> Upgrade Agents -> Post Agent Upgrade Tasks -> Sign-off Agent
Results to see job status
Job Name : CLEANUP_12CR2_AGNTS
```

Once all jobs have been verified as completed, a second check should be performed to note that the sign-off status has been received on each of the agents in question:

```
>emcli get_signoff_status

Showing for each job

Job Name Status Total Agents Started Ended

-------- ------ ------------ ------- -----

CLEANUP_12CR2_AGNTS Success 2 2013-11-21 17:08:30 CST
2013-11-21 17:08:44 CST
```

```
Note that the sign-off doesn't remove the old agent home. We will now do this through an EM CLI host
command once logged in:
>emcli execute_hostcmd –cmd="rm -rf /u01/oracle/agent12c/core/12.1.0.2.0" -targets="remote-
host:host"
```

This command will remove the previous, unused directory home from each host it is run against.

The goal of these examples is to show you very simple commands that performed several usually manual steps, thus easing the demands on the administrator. Anyone who reads through the actual steps that were required to be performed by the DBA on six servers, including verifying success and then removing the previous installation, will realize the power behind the EM CLI job-submission option.

Export/Import Capabilities for Information Publisher Reports

BI Publisher (BIP) now comes standard as an integrated part of Release 4 (12.1.0.4). With this change, Information Publisher Reports (IP Reports) are still supported, but migration to BIP is recommended.

Any report requires significant development time, and the ability to export and import it through the EM CLI is incredibly beneficial; this is no different than for your existing IP Reports. For this example, we will first list then export an IP Report named "Exadata Summary Report":

```
>emcli get_reports –owner="KPOTVIN"
```

From the list of reports owned by "KPOTVIN," we can choose one named EXADATA_SUMMARY_REPORT and export it:

```
>emcli export_report -title="Exadata Summary Report" -owner="KPOTVIN" -output_file="$OMS_HOME/
reports/exadata_summary.xml"
```

This report will now be found in the $OMS_HOME/reports directory, and the file will be named exadata_summary for easy identification.

To then import this report, the following is done:

```
>emcli import_report -files="$OMS_HOME/reports/exadata_summary.xml"
```

Exporting a BIP report is currently performed via the console and by exporting the files to local files.

Store Definition Library in Software Library

Storing definition files in the software library makes complete sense. No one wants to continue to create and retain multiple copies of the same definition file (a.k.a. response file). By implementing a software library, there is less concern about version control as this can be managed as part of the feature.

Creating a definition file is a simple process:

```
>emcli get_procedures -type=DBPROV
```

This will create a list of all provisioning procedures that can then be used to create a definition file; this will be used with a deployment or provisioning verb call. This definition file contains all targets and procedural steps. To use it as a "shortcut" versus writing out all of the tasks (like a response file eliminates similar work for a database configuration assistant [dbca] silent run) saves time and extra effort.

You can "describe" or list out the commands and information to an output file with the following command:

```
>emcli describe_procedure_input -procedure=B35E10B1F427B4EEE040578CD78179DC > newoutputfile.
properties
```

This command will create a file named "newoutputfile.properties" in the software library directory based on the procedure GUID listed in the command.

You can then open the file with VI or another editor, make whatever changes required for targets and so forth, and save it; next, upload it back into the software library:

```
>emcli save_procedure_input –name=Prov_db12cR1_temp -procedure="DB12cR1 Template" -owner="KPOTVIN"
-input_file=data:$OMS_HOME/sw_files/ newoutputfile.properties
```

The file is now uploaded to the software library and can be downloaded for future use, or can simply be used as is.

Oracle Extensibility Exchange

Oracle's Extensibility Exchange is a cloud repository (library) to which Oracle and partners have contributed scripts, plug-ins, and other Enterprise Manager entities for download. The Extensibility Exchange can be accessed via a web browser at the following link (Figure 7-12): http://www.oracle.com/goto/emextensibility.

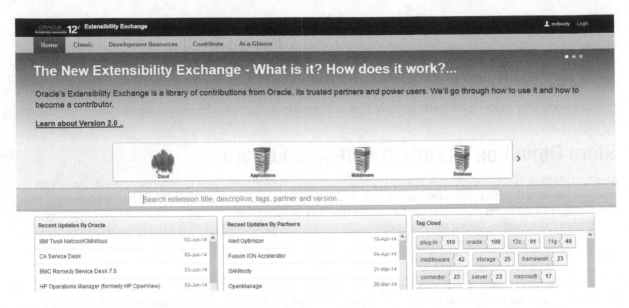

Figure 7-12. *Main page for Oracle's Extensibility Exchange, version 2.0*

The benefit of having the Extensibility Exchange is similar to that of having a provisioning library, just on a global scale. It allows EM12c professionals to share their knowledge and expertise with the rest of the OEM community. It offers solutions to those in the community, saving them time and resources that would have been otherwise wasted recreating code that others have already spent valuable time originating.

The desire to reuse Enterprise Manager entities, such as scripts, plugins, and patch plans, quickly became apparent, and there were requests for this functionality from a number of power users. No one likes to reinvent the wheel, and with the Extensibility Exchange the EM12c software library is taken to the next level. The source of available entities is no longer local to the EM12c repository, but is now available to anyone with browser access; contributions from the power users throughout the Oracle community are also available.

The future of the Extensibility Exchange is wide open with the release of version 2.0 in June 2014. As Enterprise Manager's features are enhanced, new offloading and export features are discovered, along with new scripting methods. As we do more and more within the EM CLI, we plan on seeing more Jython and JSON scripts that will encompass most of what we now do with the database environment. However, with the move to mobile, who knows what will be dreamed up with ADF (Application Development Forms) and APEX, all supported within EM12c and scripted as part of deployment through the EM CLI. Soon it won't just be plug-ins and scripts, but possibly full suites of monitoring entities that are available through the Extensibility Exchange.

To gain a better understanding of the features, we can log into the Extensibility Exchange via a web browser. The header on the page offers the user great information on upcoming Enterprise Manager training and informational events (Figure 7-13). There is also a link if one wants to proceed to the site to gain more information or register for an event.

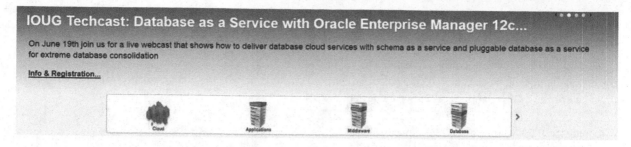

Figure 7-13. *Header page with event information and top categories on the Extensibility Exchange website*

Categories, ordered by popularity and number of entities, are shown in Figure 7-14 in the event header.

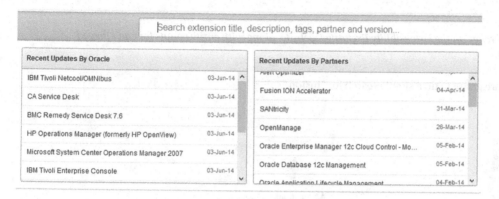

Figure 7-14. *Search bar and recent updates list of plug-ins and entities created by both Oracle and partners on the Extensibility Exchange website*

The search option is both helpful and easy to use. Simply type in a keyword and it goes to work to find all entities in the Exchange that have that term in its title.

Instead of doing a search, you can scroll to the bottom of the page to peruse the recently updated extensions in the library by Oracle, by partners, and/or by "tags," as shown in Figure 7-15. Tags are search words that can be used to offer a link button that will take you quickly to all entities or plug-ins that meet that "tagged" search.

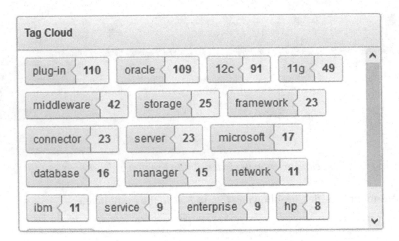

Figure 7-15. *Tagged searches on the Extensibility Exchange website, along with entity counts for each tagged search term*

In Figure 7-16, we are going to do a simple search for "fusion."

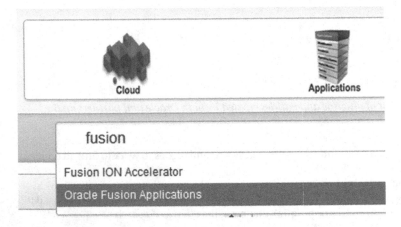

Figure 7-16. *Search bar view for the Extensibility Exchange, along with quick search results in response to keyword entry*

As you can see, the keyword "fusion" shows results immediately. For our example, we'll choose "Oracle Fusion Applications."

This takes us to the page for the entities that match our search (Figure 7-17), and we can then chose from the dropdown:.

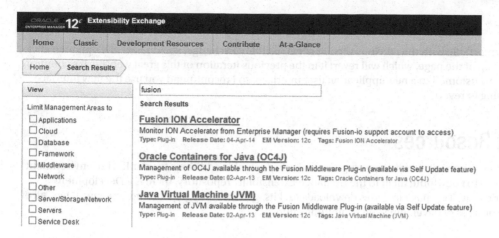

Figure 7-17. *Secondary search page from keyword entries that shows list of available plug-ins (i.e., "entities") to view or download*

Extensibility Exchange

By clicking on the first of the extensions found in a search, we are taken to the content details for the Fusion ION Accelerator plug-in (Figure 7-18).

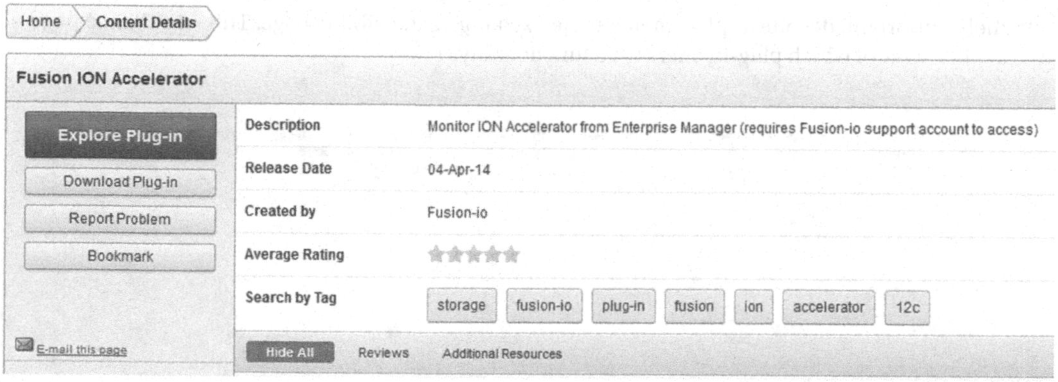

Figure 7-18. *View of access page for the Fusion ION Accelorator plug-in, which displays documentation, download, reporting, and bookmark links*

Notice that you can read the full documentation on the plug-in (Explore Plug-in), download it, report a problem if one is experienced with the plug-in, or bookmark it for later reference via a web browser.

For the future enhancement of the site, also remember to come back and rate the plug-in if you do end up downloading it. It's very valuable to other users of the Extensibility Exchange to receive feedback.

If you choose to download a plug-in and it's from Oracle, it will take you to Oracle or to the partner's page to access the download options.

Classic View

Now, if you are more comfortable with the previous version of Extensibility Exchange, you do have the option to click on the Classic tab at the top of the page, which will revert it to the previous iteration of this great website. It's common to need time to become accustomed to a new application user interface, so I recommend you use the new interface for a while before choosing to revert.

Development Resources

If your environment possesses metric extensions, plug-ins, and other valuable additions to your EM12c environment and you'd like to learn how to contribute them to the Exchange Extensibility repository, there is a Development Resources page to explain how. This page includes downloads for kits, guides, white papers, and screenwatches, all of which help simplify the process of developing and submitting entities.

Contribute

Once you have completed proper development of an entity to submit to the Extensibility Exchange, the form on the Contribute tab must be filled out. Once this is completed, click Create. Oracle will proceed to validate your contribution and then add it to the Extensibility Exchange catalog.

At a Glance

The last tab is extremely important, despite its placement on the Exchange Extensibility page. This At a Glance page (Figure 7-19) gives a quick view of which plug-in offers what functionality.

	Contributor	Target (Oracle or 3rd Party System)	Management Area	Provides Monitoring	Provides Configuration Management	Provides Patching & Provisioning	Provides Deep Performance Diagnostics	Enables Testing	Enables Private Cloud	Includes Out-of-Box Reports	Additional Purchase Required
	Blue Medora	Ping Probe	Network	✔	-	-	-	-	-	✔	✔
	Oracle	IBM DB2 Database	Database	✔	-	-	-	-	-	-	✔
	Oracle	Oracle ZFS Storage Appliance	Storage	✔	-	-	-	-	-	✔	-
	Oracle	EMC CLARiiON	Storage	✔	-	-	-	-	-	-	-
	Oracle	JBoss Application Server	Middleware	✔	✔	-	✔	-	-	-	✔
	Oracle	IBM WebSphere MQ	Middleware	✔	-	-	-	-	-	-	✔
	Oracle	Apache Tomcat	Middleware	✔	-	-	✔	-	-	-	✔

Figure 7-19. The "At a Glance" tab and the impressive comparison feature for plug-ins

It also offers a great search feature, including filters and comparison options for the different plug-ins (Figure 7-20).

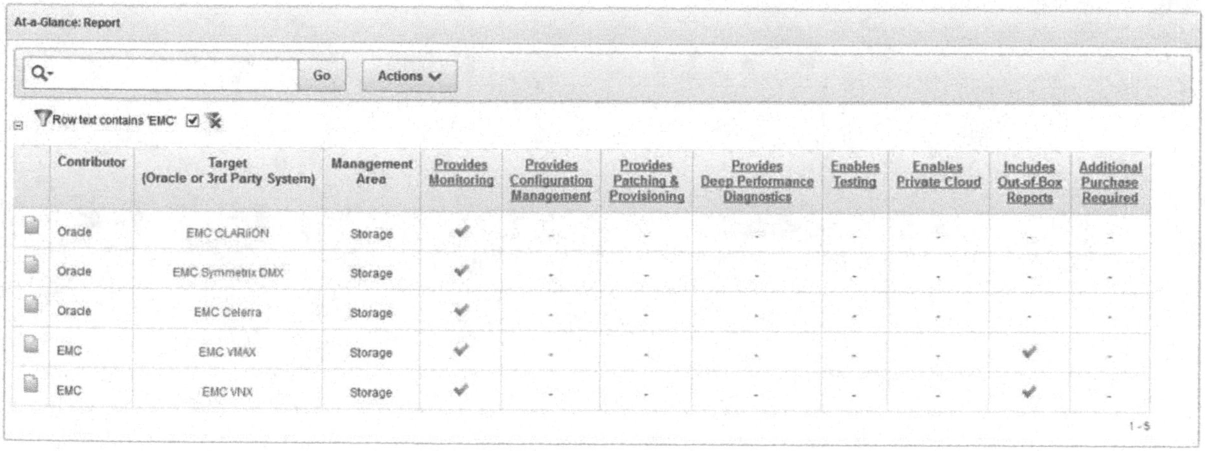

Figure 7-20. *Distinct search results and comparisons of "EMC" plug-ins, displaying which plug-ins have out-of-the-box reports included*

In this figure we perform a quick search for EMC plug-ins, and two provide "out-of-the-box" reports, so if this is a requirement of the plug-in you need, this page would quickly pinpoint you to the desired entities.

Summary

The software library is your own internal repository for entities used by the EM12c environment. The ability to also have a global software library in the Extensibility Exchange offers the Enterprise Manager the ability to share entities that they would have previously had to design themselves.

In this chapter, we discussed why you are required to have the software library configured before you're able to use many of the features of the EM12c console, including provisioning and EM CLI scripting features. We demonstrate how to configure some more-advanced features and how they benefit your day-to-day demands.

We also go into the powerful Extensibility Exchange website. This is Oracle's library of entities that allow Oracle, Oracle partners, and power users just like you to develop, test, ensure quality of, and then share entities with the Oracle community to the benefit of everyone. Providing everyone a one-stop location to view, try out, and then review plug-ins, metric extensions, and future entities is an incredible way the Oracle community can share its wealth of skills in the industry with each other.

■ ■ ■

## CHAPTER 8

Sample EM CLI Scripts

Throughout this book we've shown you how to use EM CLI to manage your OEM environment, including using the command line,. I scripting option, which uses JSON and Jython.

This chapter contains some sample scripts for you to adapt to your environment.

> Section 1: Function Library and Shell Scripts

> Section 2: EM CLI and Veritas Cluster Services

> Section 3: Essential OMS Server-Management Scripts

> Section 4: EM CLI Scripting and Interactive Scripts

Section 1: Function Library and Shell Scripts

Chapter 5 explored various ways you could apply EM CLI with shell scripts. This section expands on those solutions and provides you with sample scripts you can use in your environment.

The samples in this chapter have been edited for clarity, mostly by removing formatting options for echo statements and redirections to log files. Two of the most important things you must provide in your scripts are clear instructions for attended online use and complete log files for unattended execution through Cron or another job scheduler like OEM.

Command-Line Inputs

The use of validated input values provides scalability and ease of use. Before you deploy your scripts, consider adding and testing this important capability.

Nearly all of the scripts in this section require one or more input variables at the command line, often simply the target name. Variables passed at the command line are represented in the body of the script in the order they appear on the command line. The executable file is represented as $0, the first string after that is $1, and so forth. For example, you could have an entry like this:

```
./oem_target_blackout.sh orcla
```

This example translates variable $0 as the script name for oem_target_blackout.sh and $1 for the database name. The logic within the scripts should verify that required command-line inputs are not null or that they exit with a clear error statement telling the user or the log file what went wrong. You'll see several examples of this technique in the sample scripts.

Evidence of Life

Every shell script you develop should be executable at the command line for testing one-off runs, and should also be executable through a scheduler like Cron without any modification. Resist the temptation to use two versions of the same script to enable both modes of operation. This can turn into a maintenance nightmare as the complexity of your environment grows. Instead, test for a live user session by looking at the nature of the session that is calling the script. At run-time, a file system entry for each terminal session will be made in the /dev directory for each live user connection. TTY is an old term for **Teletype Session**—your terminal session. Cronned executions aren't called from a terminal, of course, so there is no /dev/tty associated with those executions.

Test for the existence of a TTY session with an if statement and set your runtime variables accordingly. For instance, if your script requires that the database name be passed on the command line, you will respond to missing inputs differently for an attended session than you would for a cronned/scheduled session:

```
if [ ${1} -eq 0 ]; then
  if tty -s; then
      read -p "Please provide the name of the database: " thisSID
  else
      echo "The database name was not provided on the command line"  >>runtime.log
      exit
   fi
fi
```

This type of session checking was removed from the example scripts for clarity.

Sample Function Library

This function library is sourced by many of the shell scripts found in the remainder of this section. It can also be sourced for immediate use in a terminal session, or sourced for use in any other shell script.

Sample Script: emcli_functions.lib

```
#!/bin/sh
#/* vim: set filetype=sh : */
# ============================================================================
# File:          emcli_functions.lib
# Purpose:   Shell script functions for common emcli tasks
# File permission: This file is sourced and never executed
# Echo statements: Formatting for echoed statements has been removed for this
#                           scripting sample to keep the logic clear. Be kind to your
#                           users and add white space liberally in your own copy
# ============================================================================
# The SysmanPassword variable is used in a single place to call your proprietary
# password encryption solution, or in a single location to record the SYSMAN
# password for use in your scripts and within the functions in this library.
# It is strongly recommended that you implement a more secure solution such as encryption/decryption
# through Java or another tool
# ----------------------------------------------------------------------------

SysmanPassword=Sup3r_S3cr3t_PASSWORD
```

```
# ================================================================================
#  General Functions
# ================================================================================

function CleanUpFiles {
# --------------------------------------------------------------------------------
# CleanUpFiles is called at the beginning of every script to ensure that older
# copies of temporary workfiles are removed to start fresh
# CleanUpFiles is also called by the ExitCleanly function to clean up the
# --------------------------------------------------------------------------------
# files when script execution is complete
# ................................................................................

[ $WORKFILE ] && rm -f ${WORKFILE}
[ $WORKFILE01 ] && rm -f ${WORKFILE01}
[ $WORKFILE02 ] && rm -f ${WORKFILE02}
}

function ExitCleanly {
# --------------------------------------------------------------------------------
# ExitCleanly is called whenever a script is instructed to exit, whether the
# script ended in success or failure. A clean server is a happy server
# --------------------------------------------------------------------------------

echo "Ending emcli session ..."
emcli logout
CleanUpFiles
echo ""
exit 0
}

function GetAgentNames {
# --------------------------------------------------------------------------------
# As it says in the echo statement, GetAgentNames can be used to list all
# targets of the oracle_emd target type known to OEM
# --------------------------------------------------------------------------------

emcli login -user=sysman -pass="${SysmanPassword}"
echo "Getting the names of all EM agents from OMS ..."
emcli get_targets | grep oracle_emd | sort -u | awk '{ print $4 }'
}

function GetTargetName {
# --------------------------------------------------------------------------------
# This function should be used by any script or function to find
# the exact of a database. If the database isn't known to OEM it returns a
# clear failure message.
# You could easily adapt GetTargetName to find host or agent names
```

```
# --------------------------------------------------------------------------
# Calling script must pass the database name as variable thisSID
# --------------------------------------------------------------------------

emcli login -user=sysman -pass="${SysmanPassword}"
echo "Getting the exact target name for $thisSID from OMS ..."
if [ `emcli get_targets -targets="oracle_database" | grep -i ${thisSID} | wc -l` -gt 0 ]; then
    thisTARGET=`emcli get_targets -targets="oracle_database" -format="name:csv" \
              | grep -i ${thisSID} | cut -d, -f4`
    echo "\t${thisTARGET}"
else
    echo "Sorry, ${thisSID} database is not in the OEM repository"
    ExitCleanly
fi
}


# ==========================================================================
#  Blackout Functions
# ==========================================================================

function CreateBlackout {
# --------------------------------------------------------------------------
# This function was illustrated in Chapter 5 as a method of creating a six-hour
# long blackout on a database target. Adapt the timezone for your environment.
# Consider writing a similar function of entire hosts or an oracle_sys target
# --------------------------------------------------------------------------
# Calling script must provide a name for the blackout as BO_NAME and the
# database target name as thisSID
# --------------------------------------------------------------------------

GetTargetName

echo "Creating blackout named '${BO_NAME}' ..."

if [ `emcli get_blackouts | grep ${BO_NAME} | wc -l` -gt 0 ]; then
    echo "Found an existing blackout named ${BO_NAME}"
    echo "That blackout will be stopped and deleted prior to starting the new one"
    emcli stop_blackout -name="${BO_NAME}"
    emcli delete_blackout -name="${BO_NAME}"
fi

emcli create_blackout -name="${BO_NAME}" \
    -add_targets=${thisTARGET:oracle_database \
    -schedule="duration::360;tzinfo:specified;tzregion:America/Los_Angeles" \
    -reason="Scripted blackout for maintenance or refresh"

sleep 5

echo "Getting blackout information for '${BO_NAME}' ..."
emcli get_blackout_details -name="${BO_NAME}"
}
```

```
function EndBlackout {
# -------------------------------------------------------------------------------
# This function was illustrated in Chapter 5 as a method of stopping and deleting
# an OEM blackout.
# -------------------------------------------------------------------------------
# Calling script must provide a name for the blackout as BO_NAME
# -------------------------------------------------------------------------------

GetTargetName

echo "Stopping blackout '${BO_NAME}' ..."
emcli stop_blackout -name="${BO_NAME}"

echo "Deleting blackout '${BO_NAME}' ..."
emcli delete_blackout -name="${BO_NAME}"
}


# ================================================================================
#  Agent Synchronization
# ================================================================================

function ResyncUnreachableAgents {
# -------------------------------------------------------------------------------
# This function requires no input values to resync all agents found to be in
# an Unreachable state.
#
# Underlying conditions may exist that prevent an individual agent from
# being resync'd, so check agent status after executing this function.
# Only one attempt will be made to resync each agent to prevent an infinite
# loop when problem agents are encountered
#
# This function and SecureAllAgents are written for execution from the command
# line by sourcing this library file and then calling the function by name
#
#    Examples:
#        . emcli_functions.lib
#        ResyncUnreachableAgents
#
#        . emcli_functions.lib
#        SecureAllAgents
# -------------------------------------------------------------------------------

WORKFILE01=/tmp/oem_resyncagents.tmp

CleanUpFiles

emcli login -user=sysman -pass="${SysmanPassword}"
```

```
echo "Getting the target name for unreachable agents ..."
if [ `emcli get_targets -targets="oracle_emd" | grep Unreach | awk '{ print $5 }' | wc -l` -gt 0 ];
then
    echo "Creating a list of agents in an Unreachable state"
    emcli get_targets -targets="oracle_emd" | grep Unreachable | awk '{ print $5 }' >${WORKFILE01}
    if [ `cat ${WORKFILE01} | wc -l` -gt 0 ]; then
        for thisAGENT in `cat ${WORKFILE01}`; do
            echo "Attempting to resync ${thisAGENT}"
            echo "This will take quite a while, so please be patient"
            emcli resyncAgent -agent="${thisAGENT}"
        done
    else
        echo "There are currently no unreachable agents"
    fi
else
    echo "There are currently no unreachable agents"
fi

ExitCleanly
}

function SecureAllAgents {
# ----------------------------------------------------------------------------------------
# As the name suggests, this function will secure all your agents using the
# preferred credentials for their host.
# ----------------------------------------------------------------------------------------

WORKFILE01=/tmp/oem_secure_agents.tmp

CleanUpFiles

emcli login -user=sysman -pass="${SysmanPassword}"

emcli get_targets | grep oracle_emd | sort -u | awk '{ print $4 }' >${WORKFILE01}

emcli secure_agents -agt_names_file=${WORKFILE01} -use_pref_creds

ExitCleanly
}

# ================================================================================
# User Account Credentials
# ================================================================================

function SetDBUserCredential {
# ----------------------------------------------------------------------------------------
# This function will set the normal database preferred credentials to use the
# SYSMAN password defined at the top of this file.
```

```
# -----------------------------------------------------------------------------
# Calling script must provide the database name as thisSID
# -----------------------------------------------------------------------------

emcli set_credential \
      -target_type=oracle_database \
      -target_name=${thisSID} \
      -credential_set=DBCredsNormal \
      -columns="username:dbsnmp;password:${SysmanPassword};role:Normal"
}

function SetUserCredential {
# -----------------------------------------------------------------------------
# This function will execute the SetDBUserCredential from the command line
# -----------------------------------------------------------------------------
# You could supplement the failure logic with a read statement to prompt
# for the database name
# -----------------------------------------------------------------------------

if [ ${#1} -gt 0 ]; then
   thisSID=${1}
   SetDBUserCredential
else
   echo "The database name was not set on the command line"
   echo "  syntax:  SetDBUserCredential [database name]
   exit 1
fi
}
```

Function-Related Shell Scripts

The scripts in this section call or rely on the function described earlier. In each case, the function library is sourced, input values from the command line are evaluated, and key input parameters needed by the functions are set. Notice the simplicity of these scripts. All of the "serious" logic exists in the function library, so when a new script is created you can limit your debugging to just the new code.

Sample Script: emcli_start_blackout.ksh

```
#!/bin/ksh
# Thus script is written for Korn shell. You must adapt the 'read' statements to use Bash
#
# =============================================================================
#  File:              emcli_start_blackout.ksh
#  Purpose:        Create and initiate an OEM blackout
#  Parameters:  Database name
# =============================================================================
# Enter the path to your shell script repository for OEM
FUNCTION_LIB=< Your shared script directory>/emcli_functions.lib

# WORKFILE is one of several file name variables cleaned up by the function library
export WORKFILE=/tmp/create_em_blackout_$PPID.lst
```

```ksh
# -------------------------------------------------------------------------------
#  Run-time Procedure
# -------------------------------------------------------------------------------
# Source the function library
. ${FUNCTION_LIB}

# Verify that SID was passed on command line
if [ ${#1} -eq 0 ]; then
   if tty -s; then
      read thisSID? "Please provide the name of the database: "
  else
      echo "The database name was not provided on the command line"
      ExitCleanly
   fi
   read thisSID?"Enter the name of the database to be monitored:   "
else
   thisSID=`print $@ | awk '{print$NF}' | tr '[A-Z]' '[a-z]'`
fi

BO_NAME=scripted_blackout_${thisSID}

CleanUpFiles
CreateBlackout
ExitCleanly
```

Sample Script: emcli_stop_blackout.ksh

```ksh
#!/bin/ksh
# ==============================================================================
#   File:           emcli_stop_blackout.ksh
#   Purpose:        Stop and delete a named OEM blackout
#   Parameters:  Database name
# ==============================================================================
# Enter the path to your shell script repository  for OEM
FUNCTION_LIB=< Your shared script directory>/emcli_functions.lib

# WORKFILE is one of several file name variables cleaned up by the function library
export WORKFILE=/tmp/create_em_blackout_$PPID.lst

# -------------------------------------------------------------------------------
#  Run-time Procedure
# -------------------------------------------------------------------------------
# Source the function library
. ${FUNCTION_LIB}

# Verify that SID was passed on command line
if [ ${#1} -eq 0 ]; then
   if tty -s; then
      read thisSID?"Please provide the name of the database: "
  else
      echo "The database name was not provided on the command line"
      ExitCleanly
```

```
    fi
    read thisSID?"Enter the name of the database to be monitored again:   "
else
    thisSID=`print $@ | awk '{print$NF}' | tr '[A-Z]' '[a-z]'`
fi

BO_NAME=scripted_blackout_${thisSID}

CleanUpFiles
EndBlackout
ExitCleanly
```

Section 2: EM CLI and Veritas Cluster Server

Veritas Cluster Servers (VCS)[1] are robust fail-over mechanisms deployed as an alternative to RAC One-Node. With VCS, critical resources like database instances are identified and monitored. If a failure is noticed, VCS will unmount drives containing the binaries and database files, remount them on the other node of a cluster, and restart the services.

OEM agents must be installed on a static drive on each host within the cluster. They never fail-over with the VCS resource group because they are strictly associated with a single host. This poses a problem with VCS fail overs. How do you keep track of the targets when the database, its Oracle home, and all of its files move to another host?

■ **Tip** Many consider it a best practice on VCS to install the agents on the virtual hostname. Refer to "How to Install 12c Agent on Virtual Hostname / Virtual IP Address?" (Doc ID 1469995.1) for details.

The EM CLI `relocate_targets` verb transfers responsibility for target tracking to another agent when the targets are relocated by the VCS. This section describes how that process works before showing you the shell script itself.

Program Logic

This script gathers data from the environment and decides which targets are moving and which agents are affected. This script's scalability and flexibility come from queries of three systems: the VCS cluster, the OEM repository, and the EM agent. Note that syntax is slightly different for relocating responsibility between agents for database and listener targets. We'll generate a separate set of workfiles for generating the EM CLI argfile that actually performs the work.

Veritas Cluster Server

VCS clusters are organized into groups that drill down to the individual database and listener targets. The hosts in the cluster are at the highest level. VCS heartbeats monitor one or more critical resources on the active node and when necessary relocate all the members[2] of a group from the current ONLINE node to the other node that is currently OFFLINE. We'll use this knowledge to determine the host and agent names we need to manage.

---

[1]http://www.symantec.com/cluster-server.

[2]Members on a database server typically include databases and listeners using the same Oracle home. The drives related to these targets are all members of the group. Filesystems containing the Oracle base, the archive destination, the oradata filesystems, and other related data are all included in the fail-over group.

Since EM agents can only monitor targets that run from the same host (or Oracle cluster), we need to carefully determine which targets are related to the VCS group being failed-over. Those database and listener targets are the only targets eligible for relocation through EM CLI. We'll use a second set of VCS query results to decide which EM targets need to be relocated.

For example, let's say you have two Oracle installations, each with their own Oracle base filesystem. Each base, or home, contains all the files required to support its own targets, of course, and many databases and listeners may use those homes. They are all members of one fail-over group. Let's say the groups are named QUAL and TEST.

- The QUAL group has one database named alexis_q with a listener named LSNRQ.

- TEST group has three databases, alexis_t1, alexis_t2, and alexis_t3, and a shared listener named LSNRT.

- Alexis_q database is identified as the critical resource for the QUAL cluster group.

- All three databases in the TEST cluster group are identified as "critical resources" in the TEST cluster group.

If VCS does not receive a response back from its heartbeat against the alexis_q, all the resources in the QUAL cluster group will fail-over to the other node.

If any of three databases in the TEST node becomes unresponsive, everything on that node, including the healthy databases, will be restarted by VCS on the other node.

A VCS relocation often takes only a moment or two while the healthy members of the resource group (other databases sharing the binaries and any related listeners) are brought down, filesystems are unmounted and then re-mounted, and finally all the resources are brought up. Manual intervention is not required.

Oracle Enterprise Manager

Databases and listeners on either host may have been ignored, dropped, or simply never discovered in Enterprise Manager, so there's nothing to change in OEM. We'll check both the EM repository and the local agent to decide which targets need to be relocated.[3]

In this example, only databases alexis_q and alexis_t1 are configured for monitoring in OEM. The EM agent knows about all of them, of course, but OEM monitoring and metrics collection only apply to the first two and their respective listeners. As far as OEM is concerned, we can ignore the other two databases completely. After the relocation is complete, the agent on the new node will discover alexis_t2 and alexis_t3 as part of its own host discovery. The agent on the other node also performs regular searches for new targets, so it will essentially forget about the unmonitored databases. The EM CLI command will transfer its knowledge about the history, metric collections, and preferred credentials for alexis_q and alexis_t1. That knowledge transfer is the purpose of this exercise, after all.

Implementation

The `emcli_relocate_target_vcs.ksh` script is executed without command-line input parameters by VCS after all the other fail-over tasks are complete, including restarting the databases and listeners:

Sample Script: `emcli_relocate_target_vcs.ksh`

---

[3]In spite of its title, `relocate_target` verb does not physically relocate any targets. Its sole purpose is to transfer monitoring and metrics collection from one agent to another.

```sh
#!/bin/sh
# ==============================================================================
#  File:              emcli_relocate_target_vcs.sh
#  Purpose:     Relocate OEM agent for monitored VCS targets
#  Parameters: VCS group name required
#  Note:              Must be run as part of  VCS startup to run after fail-over
#                          to the secondary host
# ==============================================================================
# Environment tests
# ------------------------------------------------------------------------------
if [ ${#1} -eq 0 ]; then
   echo "You must pass the VCS cluster name on the command line\n\n"
   exit 1
fi

export VCSBIN=< Set to the bin directory for your VRTSvcs executables >

if [ ! -d ${VCSBIN} ]; then
   echo  "Could not locate the Veritas executables in ${VCSBIN}"
   export VCSBIN=""
   exit 1
fi


# ------------------------------------------------------------------------------
# Variables section
# ------------------------------------------------------------------------------
SCRIPTNAME=`basename ${0}`
LOCAL_HOST=`hostname | cut -d"." -f1`

# ------------------------------------------------------------------------------
# Set the ORACLE_HOME to the agent's base directory
# EM agent installs with its own jdk, so reference it in this script
# ------------------------------------------------------------------------------
export ORACLE_HOME=/u01/oracle/product/agent12c
export EMCTL_HOME=${ORACLE_HOME}/agent_inst/bin
export JAVA_HOME=${ORACLE_HOME}/core/12.1.0.3.0/jdk/bin
# ------------------------------------------------------------------------------
# The settings shown assume EM CLI binaries reside in the agent O/H
# ------------------------------------------------------------------------------

export EMCLI_HOME=${ORACLE_HOME}/emcli

# Set paths to match the values set above

export PATH=${VCS_BIN}:${PATH}
export PATH=${ORACLE_HOME}:${ORACLE_HOME}/bin:${PATH}
export PATH=${EMCTL_HOME}:${PATH}
export PATH=${JAVA_HOME}:${PATH}
export PATH=${EMCLI_HOME}:${PATH}

export PATH=${PATH}:.
export LD_LIBRARY_PATH=${ORACLE_HOME}/lib:/lib:/lib64:/usr/lib:/usr/lib64
```

```
# Set fully-qualified paths to the executables here

export EMCLI=${EMCLI_HOME}/emcli
export EMCTL=${EMCTL_HOME}/emctl
export JAVA=${JAVA_HOME}/java

export IBM_JAVA_OPTIONS=-Djava.net.preferIPv4Stack=true

# Required setting for an AIX environment

export AIXTHREAD_SCOPE=S

# ----------------------------------------------------------------------------------
# File name variables - keep these in the same order as CleanUpFiles function
# ----------------------------------------------------------------------------------
# Lists will be collected from each of source as listed and distilled into the
# final EM CLI script
#
# emcli relocate_targets verb syntax is slightly different for databases and
# listeners so we'll collect them in separate lists of targets for processing
# ----------------------------------------------------------------------------------

VCS_DATABASES=/tmp/RelocateTargetDatabases_VCS.lst
VCS_LISTENERS=/tmp/RelocateTargetListeners_VCS.lst

EMCLI_DATABASES=/tmp/RelocateTargetDatabases_EMCLI.lst
EMCLI_LISTENERS=/tmp/RelocateTargetListeners_EMCLI.lst

EMCTL_DATABASES=/tmp/RelocateTargetDatabases_EMCTL.lst
EMCTL_LISTENERS=/tmp/RelocateTargetListeners_EMCTL.lst

OEM_DATABASES=/tmp/RelocateTargetDatabases_OEM.lst
OEM_LISTENERS=/tmp/RelocateTargetListeners_OEM.lst

MOVING_DATABASES=/tmp/RelocateTargetDatabases_Moving.lst
MOVING_LISTENERS=/tmp/RelocateTargetListeners_Moving.lst

EMCLI_SCRIPT=/tmp/RelocateTarget_emcli_script.lst


#============================================================================
# Functions
#============================================================================

function CleanUpFiles {
# ----------------------------------------------------------------------------------
[ $VCS_DATABASES ] && rm -f ${VCS_DATABASES}
[ $VCS_LISTENERS ] && rm -f ${VCS_LISTENERS}
[ $EMCLI_DATABASES ] && rm -f ${EMCLI_DATABASES}
[ $EMCLI_LISTENERS ] && rm -f ${EMCLI_LISTENERS}
[ $EMCTL_DATABASES ] && rm -f ${EMCTL_DATABASES}
[ $EMCTL_LISTENERS ] && rm -f ${EMCTL_LISTENERS}
```

```
[ $OEM_DATABASES ] && rm -f ${OEM_DATABASES}
[ $OEM_LISTENERS ] && rm -f ${OEM_LISTENERS}
[ $MOVING_DATABASES ] && rm -f ${MOVING_DATABASES}
[ $MOVING_LISTENERS ] && rm -f ${MOVING_LISTENERS}
[ $EMCLI_SCRIPT ] && rm -f ${EMCLI_SCRIPT}
}

function ExitCleanly {
# --------------------------------------------------------------------------------
CleanUpFiles
exit 0
}

function ExitDirty {
# --------------------------------------------------------------------------------
CleanUpFiles
exit 1
}

function ListNicely {
# --------------------------------------------------------------------------------
for thisLINE in `cat ${thisFILE}`; do
   echo "  ${thisLINE}"
done
}

# --------------------------------------------------------------------------------
# Runtime procedure
# --------------------------------------------------------------------------------
# Time stamp for the VCS log file
# --------------------------------------------------------------------------------
echo "\n\n\n--------------------------------------------------------------------"
date
echo "--------------------------------------------------------------------\n\n\n"

CleanUpFiles

 # --------------------------------------------------------------------------------
# Gather VCS values for the members of the cluster
# --------------------------------------------------------------------------------
# Test whether VCS recognizes the cluster name you passed at the command line
# by checking for the existence of node in OFFLINE mode. From that knowledge
# we can get the name of the HAGROUP and then associate the offline and online
# nodes with the appropriate variable based on their status after the
# VCS fail-over

if [ `sudo ${VCSBIN}/hastatus -summary | grep OFFLINE | grep ${1} | wc -l` -eq 0 ]; then
    echo "\n\nThe VCS cluster ${1} does not exist on ${LOCAL_HOST}\n\n"
    ExitDirty
```

```
else
    export HAGROUP=`sudo ${VCSBIN}/hastatus -summary | grep OFFLINE | grep ${1} | awk '{ print $2 }'`
    export OFFLINE_NODE=`sudo ${VCSBIN}/hastatus -summary | grep OFFLINE | grep ${HAGROUP} | awk
'{ print $3 }'`
    if [ `sudo ${VCSBIN}/hastatus -summary | grep ONLINE | grep ${HAGROUP} | wc -l` -gt 0 ]; then
        export ONLINE_NODE=`sudo ${VCSBIN}/hastatus -summary | grep ONLINE | grep ${HAGROUP} | awk
'{ print $3 }'`
    else
        export ONLINE_NODE=`sudo ${VCSBIN}/hastatus -summary | grep PARTIAL | grep ${HAGROUP} | awk
'{ print $3 }'`
    fi
fi

# -------------------------------------------------------------------------------------
# Echo those values for the log file
# -------------------------------------------------------------------------------------
echo "\n\nVeritas Cluster names:"
echo "  VCS group                       ${HAGROUP}"
echo "  Active node after relocation    ${ONLINE_NODE}"
echo "  Offline node                    ${OFFLINE_NODE}"
echo "  Local hostname                  ${LOCAL_HOST}"

# -------------------------------------------------------------------------------------
# Select the database and listener names associated with the HAGROUP
# This list may not match the list of targets known to OEM on these hosts, so we'll compare
# them later in the script
# -------------------------------------------------------------------------------------
sudo ${VCSBIN}/hares -display -type Oracle  | grep ${HAGROUP} | awk '{ print $1 }' >${VCS_DATABASES}
sudo ${VCSBIN}/hares -display -type Netlsnr | grep ${HAGROUP} | awk '{ print $1 }' >${VCS_LISTENERS}

if [ `cat ${VCS_DATABASES} | wc -l` -gt 0 ]; then
    echo "\n\nVCS shows these databases in ${HAGROUP} group"
    thisFILE=${VCS_DATABASES}
    ListNicely
else
    echo "\n\nVCS has no databases associated with ${HAGROUP} group"
    ExitDirty
Fi

if [ `cat ${VCS_LISTENERS} | wc -l` -gt 0 ]; then
        echo "\n\nVCS shows these listeners in ${HAGROUP} group"
        thisFILE=${VCS_LISTENERS}
        ListNicely
Else
        echo "\n\nVCS has no listeners associated with ${HAGROUP} group"
fi

if [ ${OFFLINE_NODE} == ${LOCAL_HOST} ]; then
    echo "\n\nThe ${HAGROUP} group is located on the other side of the cluster"
    echo "This script must be run on the active node ${ONLINE_NODE}\n\n\n"
    ExitDirty
Fi
```

```
# -------------------------------------------------------------------------------
# Get OEM agent names, including ports, for both nodes
# Agents are always installed on a static file system and never fail over
# -------------------------------------------------------------------------------
NEW_EMD=`$EMCLI get_targets | grep ${ONLINE_NODE}  | grep oracle_emd |  awk '{print $NF }'`
OLD_EMD=`$EMCLI get_targets | grep ${OFFLINE_NODE} | grep oracle_emd |  awk '{print $NF }'`


# -------------------------------------------------------------------------------
# This string will be used several times during emcli script construction
# -------------------------------------------------------------------------------
EMCLI_AGENT_STRING=`echo "-src_agent=\"${OLD_EMD}\" -dest_agent=\"${NEW_EMD}\""`

echo "\n\nOEM names for the host targets related to this change:"
echo "  Host after relocation          ${NEW_EMD}"
echo "  Local host name                ${OLD_EMD}"


# -------------------------------------------------------------------------------
# Create and distill lists of OEM targets
# Not all targets are managed by OEM, so we need to get a list from the repository
# that we'll compare with the list from VCS
# -------------------------------------------------------------------------------

$EMCLI get_targets | grep oracle_database | awk '{print $NF}' | sort -fu >${EMCLI_DATABASES}

echo "\n\nDatabase targets managed through OEM:"
thisFILE=${EMCLI_DATABASES}
ListNicely


$EMCLI get_targets | grep oracle_listener | awk '{print $NF}' | sort -fu >${EMCLI_LISTENERS}
echo "\n\nListener targets managed through OEM:"
thisFILE=${EMCLI_LISTENERS}
ListNicely


# -------------------------------------------------------------------------------
# Now we'll do the same thing for targets known to the local EM agent. This list
# may include targets ignored or unpromoted in the repository, so we'll treat the
# agent list as a better choice. If the local agent has no targets we'll use
# the full list from the repository
# -------------------------------------------------------------------------------

$EMCTL config agent listtargets | grep oracle_database | cut -d"[" -f2 | cut -d, -f1 | sort -fu
>${EMCTL_DATABASES}
echo "\n\nLocal database targets currently associated with ${NEW_EMD}:"
thisFILE=${EMCTL_DATABASES}
ListNicely


$EMCTL config agent listtargets | grep oracle_listener | cut -d"[" -f2 | cut -d, -f1 | sort -fu
>${EMCTL_LISTENERS}
echo "\n\nLocal listener targets currently associated with ${NEW_EMD}:"
thisFILE=${EMCTL_LISTENERS}
ListNicely
```

```
# ---------------------------------------------------------------------------
# The longer list from the repository was created in case the local agent did not
# contain any targets. We'll replace the OMR list with the targets known to the
# local agent if any exist
# ---------------------------------------------------------------------------

if [ `cat ${EMCTL_DATABASES} | wc -l` -gt 0 ]; then
    cat /dev/null                           >${OEM_DATABASES}
    for thisTARGET in `cat ${EMCLI_DATABASES}`; do
        if [ `cat ${EMCTL_DATABASES} | grep -i ${thisTARGET} | wc -l` -eq 0 ]; then
            echo "${thisTARGET}"            >>${OEM_DATABASES}
        fi
    done
else
    mv -f ${EMCLI_DATABASES} ${OEM_DATABASES}
fi


# ---------------------------------------------------------------------------
# Same process happens for the listeners
# ---------------------------------------------------------------------------

if [ `cat ${EMCTL_LISTENERS} | wc -l` -gt 0 ]; then
    cat /dev/null                           >${OEM_LISTENERS}
    for thisTARGET in `cat ${EMCLI_LISTENERS}`; do
        if [ `cat ${EMCTL_LISTENERS} | grep -i ${thisTARGET} | wc -l` -eq 0 ]; then
            echo "${thisTARGET}"            >>${OEM_LISTENERS}
        fi
    done
else
    mv -f ${EMCLI_LISTENERS} ${OEM_LISTENERS}
fi


# ---------------------------------------------------------------------------
# Compare the OEM target list with the Veritas members and build emcli scripts
# ---------------------------------------------------------------------------

if [ `cat ${VCS_DATABASES} | wc -l` -gt 0 ]; then
    cat /dev/null                           >${MOVING_DATABASES}
    for thisITEM in `cat ${VCS_DATABASES}`; do
        cat ${OEM_DATABASES} | grep -i ${thisITEM} >>${MOVING_DATABASES}
    done
fi

cat /dev/null                           >${EMCLI_SCRIPT}

if [ `cat ${MOVING_DATABASES} | wc -l` -gt 0 ]; then
    echo "\n\nThese database targets will be relocated"
    thisFILE=${MOVING_DATABASES}
    ListNicely
```

```
    for thisITEM in `cat ${MOVING_DATABASES}`; do
        EMCLI_TARGET_STRING=`echo "-target_name=\"${thisITEM}\" -target_type=\"oracle_database\""`
        echo "set_standby_agent ${EMCLI_AGENT_STRING} ${EMCLI_TARGET_STRING}"  >>${EMCLI_SCRIPT}
        echo "relocate_targets  ${EMCLI_AGENT_STRING} ${EMCLI_TARGET_STRING} -copy_from_src
-force=yes" >>${EMCLI_SCRIPT}
    done
else
    echo "\n\nNo database targets need to be migrated to ${NEW_EMD}"
fi


if [ `cat ${VCS_LISTENERS} | wc -l` -gt 0 ]; then
    cat /dev/null                        >${MOVING_LISTENERS}
    for thisITEM in `cat ${VCS_LISTENERS} | sed 's/lsnr//'`; do
        cat ${OEM_LISTENERS} | grep -i ${thisITEM} >>${MOVING_LISTENERS}
    done
else
    echo "\n\nVCS has no listeners associated with ${HAGROUP} group"
fi


if [ `cat ${MOVING_LISTENERS} | wc -l` -gt 0 ]; then
    echo "\n\nThese listener targets will be relocated to ${NEW_EMD}"
    thisFILE=${MOVING_LISTENERS}
    ListNicely
    for thisITEM in `cat ${MOVING_LISTENERS}`; do
        EMCLI_TARGET_STRING=`echo "-target_name=\"${thisITEM}\" -target_type=\"oracle_listener\""`
        echo "set_standby_agent ${EMCLI_AGENT_STRING} ${EMCLI_TARGET_STRING}" >>${EMCLI_SCRIPT}
        echo "relocate_targets  ${EMCLI_AGENT_STRING} ${EMCLI_TARGET_STRING} -copy_from_src"
>>${EMCLI_SCRIPT}
    done
else
    echo "\n\nNo listener targets need to be migrated to ${NEW_EMD}"
fi

sleep 10

# -------------------------------------------------------------------------------------------
# Show the emcli to the log file and then execute it with emcli argfile
# -------------------------------------------------------------------------------------------

if [ `cat ${EMCLI_SCRIPT} | wc -l` -gt 0 ]; then
    echo "\n\nEMCLI script"
    cat ${EMCLI_SCRIPT}
    echo "\n\nEMCLI execution results"
    $EMCLI argfile ${EMCLI_SCRIPT}
fi

echo "\n\nThese targets are now tracked by the local OEM agent:\n"
$EMCTL config agent listtargets | grep -v "Cloud" | grep -v "reserved." | sort -fu
echo "\n\n\n"


ExitCleanly
```

Section 3: Essential Server-Management Scripts

The shell scripts in this section contain various uses of EM CLI, including backing up all configuration files on your OMS server and then controlling the amount of space consumed by OMS log files.

Oracle has been very good about providing these services for files they deem critical. These scripts take care of all the rest.

Configuration Backup Script

OEM backs up key OMS configuration files to the repository database. This script performs a file-level backup for those files (and several others). One should use the same shared filesystem used by the Software Library as the site of those backups.

This script only creates new backups when it determines that the source file has different content than its backup copy. If a difference exists, the old backup is renamed with a .old suffix. This provides you with another troubleshooting tool that can be particularly helpful after OMS patching. You can use file creation dates to determine which configuration files changed and then run a quick diff command to find out how they changed:

Sample Script: backup_oms_configs.ksh

```
#!/bin/ksh


#=============================================================================
# Script name  : backup_oms_configs.ksh
# Calling args : None
# Purpose      :    Backup key OMS configuration files
#=============================================================================
# Independent variables
#=============================================================================
export OMS_HOME=<Set your OMS home directory here>
export BACKUP_DIR=<Set backup destination directory here>


#=============================================================================
# Functions
#=============================================================================
function DashedBreak {
echo "\n--------------------------------------------------------------------\n"
}

function PrepareBackupDir {

SOURCE_DIR=${OMS_HOME}/${DIRNAME}
TARGET_DIR=${BACKUP_DIR}/${DIRNAME}
STAGE_DIR=${TARGET_DIR}/staging
if [ -d ${TARGET_DIR} ]; then
   echo "\n\nFound directory ${TARGET_DIR}\n\n"
else
   echo "\n\nCreating directory ${TARGET_DIR}\n\n"
   mkdir -p ${TARGET_DIR}
```

```
fi

chmod 770 ${TARGET_DIR}

if [ ! -d ${STAGE_DIR} ]; then
   mkdir ${STAGE_DIR}
fi

chmod 770 ${STAGE_DIR}
}

function BackupConfigFile {

sourceFILE=${SOURCE_DIR}/${FILENAME}
stageFILE=${TARGET_DIR}/staging/${FILENAME}
targetFILE=${TARGET_DIR}/${FILENAME}
oldFILE=${targetFILE}.old
oldZIP=${oldFILE}.zip

DashedBreak

if [ -f ${sourceFILE} ]; then
   if [ -f ${targetFILE} ]; then
      echo "\nBacking up ${sourceFILE}\n"
      cp -f ${sourceFILE} ${stageFILE}
      if [ `diff ${stageFILE} ${targetFILE} | wc -l` -gt 1 ]; then
         echo "\n\tExisting backup file will be renamed and gzipped\n"
            if [ -f ${targetFILE} ]; then
               ## Get rid of older copies of both files
               [ $oldZIP ] && rm -f ${oldZIP}
               [ $oldFILE ] && rm -f ${oldFILE}
               ## Rename and gzip the latest backup copy
               echo "\tRenaming the existing backup file\n"
               mv ${targetFILE} ${oldFILE}
               echo "\tGzipping that copy\n"
               gzip -f ${oldFILE} --fast
               chmod 600 ${oldZIP}
            fi
         echo "\nBacking up ${sourceFILE}\n"
         mv ${stageFILE} ${targetFILE}
         chmod 640 ${targetFILE}
         echo "\n\tNew backup file moved into place\n"
      else
         echo "\n\tThe current copy of ${FILENAME} is identical to the backup copy\n"
         rm -f ${stageFILE}
      fi
   else
      echo "\n\tMaking a copy of ${sourceFILE}\n"
      cp ${sourceFILE} ${targetFILE}
   fi
   echo "\n\t${sourceFILE} does not exist on this server\n\n"
```

```
fi
chmod 640 ${targetFILE}

echo "\n\tFinished\n\n"
}

# ========================================================================
#  Run-time Procedure
# ========================================================================

echo "\nBackup directories and contents before processing\n\n"
ls -lARp ${BACKUP_DIR} | grep -v "^total"

DashedBreak

# --------------------------------------------------------------------------------------
# Script sets the directory name and then lists each file
# subject to backup. The functions turn the values set as DIRNAME
# and FILENAME into source and target names for processing
# --------------------------------------------------------------------------------------

FILENAME=access.conf
   BackupConfigFile

FILENAME=mod_osso.conf
   BackupConfigFile

FILENAME=oracle_apache.conf
   BackupConfigFile

FILENAME=httpd.conf
   BackupConfigFile

FILENAME=ssl.conf
   BackupConfigFile

FILENAME=mod_oc4j.conf
   BackupConfigFile

FILENAME=dms.conf
   BackupConfigFile

# --------------------------------------------------------------------------------------

DIRNAME=Apache/jsp/conf
   PrepareBackupDir

FILENAME=ojsp.conf
   BackupConfigFile
```

```
# -------------------------------------------------------------------------------------

DIRNAME=Apache/modplsql/conf
    PrepareBackupDir

FILENAME=cache.conf
    BackupConfigFile

FILENAME=plsql.conf
    BackupConfigFile

FILENAME=dads.conf
    BackupConfigFile

# -------------------------------------------------------------------------------------

DIRNAME=Apache/oradav/conf
    PrepareBackupDir

FILENAME=oradav.conf
    BackupConfigFile

FILENAME=moddav.conf
    BackupConfigFile

# -------------------------------------------------------------------------------------

DIRNAME=datadirect/lib
    PrepareBackupDir

FILENAME=krb5.conf
    BackupConfigFile

FILENAME=JDBCDriverLogin.conf
    BackupConfigFile

# -------------------------------------------------------------------------------------

DIRNAME=dsa
    PrepareBackupDir

FILENAME=dsa.conf
    BackupConfigFile

# -------------------------------------------------------------------------------------

DIRNAME=dcm/config
    PrepareBackupDir

FILENAME=dcm.conf
    BackupConfigFile
```

```
# -----------------------------------------------------------------------------

DIRNAME=dcm/config/plugins/apache
   PrepareBackupDir

FILENAME=httpd.conf
   BackupConfigFile

# -----------------------------------------------------------------------------

DIRNAME=diagnostics/config
   PrepareBackupDir

FILENAME=logloader.xml
   BackupConfigFile

# -----------------------------------------------------------------------------

DIRNAME=iaspt/conf
   PrepareBackupDir

FILENAME=iaspt.conf
   BackupConfigFile

# -----------------------------------------------------------------------------

DIRNAME=j2ee/home/application-deployments/IsWebCacheWorking
   PrepareBackupDir

FILENAME=jazn-data.xml
   BackupConfigFile

# -----------------------------------------------------------------------------

DIRNAME=j2ee/home/application-deployments/portletapp
   PrepareBackupDir

FILENAME=jazn-data.xml
   BackupConfigFile

FILENAME=orion-application.xml
   BackupConfigFile

# -----------------------------------------------------------------------------

DIRNAME=j2ee/OC4J_EM/config
   PrepareBackupDir

FILENAME=jazn-data.xml
   BackupConfigFile

FILENAME=jazn.xml
   BackupConfigFile
```

```
# ---------------------------------------------------------------------------

DIRNAME=j2ee/OC4J_EMPROV/application-deployments/em
   PrepareBackupDir

FILENAME=jazn-data.xml
   BackupConfigFile

# ---------------------------------------------------------------------------

DIRNAME=j2ee/OC4J_EMPROV/application-deployments/EMAgentPush
   PrepareBackupDir

FILENAME=jazn-data.xml
   BackupConfigFile

FILENAME=orion-application.xml
   BackupConfigFile

# ---------------------------------------------------------------------------

DIRNAME=j2ee/OC4J_EMPROV/config
   PrepareBackupDir

FILENAME=jazn-data.xml
   BackupConfigFile

FILENAME=jazn.xml
   BackupConfigFile

# ---------------------------------------------------------------------------

DIRNAME=j2ee/OCMRepeater/application-deployments/OCMRepeater
   PrepareBackupDir

FILENAME=jazn-data.xml
   BackupConfigFile

# ---------------------------------------------------------------------------

DIRNAME=j2ee/OCMRepeater/config
   PrepareBackupDir

FILENAME=jazn-data.xml
   BackupConfigFile

FILENAME=jazn.xml
   BackupConfigFile
```

```
# -----------------------------------------------------------------------------

DIRNAME=ldap/das
    PrepareBackupDir

FILENAME=oiddas.conf
    BackupConfigFile

# -----------------------------------------------------------------------------

DIRNAME=opmn/conf
    PrepareBackupDir

FILENAME=ons.conf
    BackupConfigFile

FILENAME=opmn.xml
    BackupConfigFile

# -----------------------------------------------------------------------------

DIRNAME=sysman/config
    PrepareBackupDir

FILENAME=httpd_em.conf
    BackupConfigFile

FILENAME=agentpush.conf
    BackupConfigFile

FILENAME=agent_download.conf
    BackupConfigFile

FILENAME=emoms.properties
    BackupConfigFile

# -----------------------------------------------------------------------------

DIRNAME=sysman/emd
    PrepareBackupDir

FILENAME=lastupld.xml
    BackupConfigFile

FILENAME=targets.xml
    BackupConfigFile
```

```
# -------------------------------------------------------------------------------------

DIRNAME=sysman/j2ee/applications/Oc4jDcmServlet/META-INF
    PrepareBackupDir

FILENAME=application.xml
    BackupConfigFile

FILENAME=orion-application.xml
    BackupConfigFile

FILENAME=jazn-data.xml
    BackupConfigFile

FILENAME=principals.xml
    BackupConfigFile

# -------------------------------------------------------------------------------------

DIRNAME=sysman/j2ee/applications/Oc4jDcmServlet/Oc4jDcmServlet/WEB-INF
    PrepareBackupDir

FILENAME=orion-web.xml
    BackupConfigFile

FILENAME=web.xml
    BackupConfigFile

# -------------------------------------------------------------------------------------

DIRNAME=sysman/j2ee/application-deployments/Oc4jDcmServlet
    PrepareBackupDir

FILENAME=orion-application.xml
    BackupConfigFile

FILENAME=orion-web.xml
    BackupConfigFile

# -------------------------------------------------------------------------------------

DIRNAME=sysman/webapps/emd/online_help
    PrepareBackupDir

FILENAME=ohwconfig.xml
    BackupConfigFile
```

```
# ---------------------------------------------------------------------------

DIRNAME=uix
    PrepareBackupDir

FILENAME=uix.conf
    BackupConfigFile

# ---------------------------------------------------------------------------

DIRNAME=wcs/config
    PrepareBackupDir

FILENAME=wcs_httpd.conf
    BackupConfigFile

# ---------------------------------------------------------------------------

DIRNAME=webcache
    PrepareBackupDir

FILENAME=internal.xml
    BackupConfigFile

DashedBreak

echo "\nBackup directories and contents after processing\n\n"
ls -lARp ${BACKUP_DIR} | grep -v "^total"
```

Transitory File Cleanup Script

Oracle Management Server generates logs for each of its components, from the WebLogic server down to the EM agent on the host. Preinstalled rotations and file cleanup are very helpful where they exist, but some of the files aren't managed that way. It's up to you to keep your server tidy.

This script works its way through the log directories on an OMS server. Each file is evaluated for how long it has been idle. Older files are then removed:

```
#!/bin/ksh
#===============================================================================
#  Script name  : log_blaster_oms.ksh
#  Calling args : None
#  Purpose      : Clean up logs files for OMS
#                      References come from MOS Note 1445743.1
#===============================================================================
#  Independent variables
#==============================================================
# Set these variables to your local directory settings
# The EM_INSTANCE_HOME is typically MIDDLEWARE_HOME/gc_inst
EM_INSTANCE_HOME=

WORKFILE=/tmp/logblaster_oms_workfile1.lst
```

```
#=====================================================================
#  Functions
# =====================================================================

function CleanUpFiles {
# ----------------------------------------------------------------------------------------------------

[ $WORKFILE ] && rm -f ${WORKFILE}
}

function TrimThisFile {
# ----------------------------------------------------------------------------------------------------
if [ -d ${thisDIR} ]; then
    if [ `find ${thisDIR} -name ${thisFILE} | wc -l` -gt 0 ]; then
        NEW_FILE=${thisDIR}/${thisFILE}
        OLD_FILE=${thisDIR}/${thisFILE}_old
        LAST_DATE=`tail -1 ${NEW_FILE} | awk '{ print $1,$2,$3 }'`
        echo "\nTrimming ${NEW_FILE}"
        echo "Entries older than ${LAST_DATE} will be removed\n"
        mv -f ${NEW_FILE} ${OLD_FILE}
        cat ${OLD_FILE} | grep "${LAST_DATE}" >${NEW_FILE}
            if [ `cat ${NEW_FILE} | wc -l` -gt 0 ]; then
                rm -f ${OLD_FILE}
            else
                mv -f ${OLD_FILE} ${NEW_FILE}
            fi
    fi
    echo "\n\n"
else
    echo "\nDirectory ${thisDIR} not found\n\n"
fi
}

function SweepThese {
# ----------------------------------------------------------------------------------------------------
if [ -d ${thisDIR} ]; then
    find ${thisDIR} -name ${thisFILE} -mtime +${thisAGE} >${WORKFILE}
    if [ `cat ${WORKFILE} | wc -l` -gt 0 ]; then
        echo "\nCleaning up ${thisDIR} directory"
        for thisTRASH in `cat ${WORKFILE}`; do
            echo"\tRemoving ${thisTRASH}"
            rm -f ${thisTRASH}
        done
    else
        echo "\nNo files over ${thisAGE} days old matching"
        echo "${thisDIR}/${thisFILE}"
    fi
    echo "\n\n"
else
    echo "\nDirectory ${thisDIR} not found\n\n"
fi
}
```

151

```
# ----------------------------------------------------------------------------------
#  Run-time procedure
# ----------------------------------------------------------------------------------

CleanUpFiles

# ----------------------------------------------------------------------------------
# The webtier directory name is pulled from the environment
# Typically the value discovered  OMS1, but it may be different
# ----------------------------------------------------------------------------------

WEBTIERn=`ls ${EM_INSTANCE_HOME} | grep WebTier`

OHSn=`ls ${EM_INSTANCE_HOME}/${WEBTIERn}/diagnostics/logs/OHS | grep ohs`

# ----------------------------------------------------------------------------------
# Retention for this directory is set for seven days through thisAGE variable
# ----------------------------------------------------------------------------------

thisDIR=${EM_INSTANCE_HOME}/${WEBTIERn}/diagnostics/logs/OHS/${OHSn}
   thisAGE=7

thisFILE="em_upload_http_access_log.*"
   SweepThese

thisFILE="em_upload_https_access_log.*"
   SweepThese

thisFILE="access_log.*"
   SweepThese

thisFILE="ohs*.log"
   SweepThese

thisFILE="console~OHS*.log*"
   SweepThese

thisFILE="mod_wl_ohs.log"
   TrimThisFile

# ----------------------------------------------------------------------------------

DOMAIN_SERVERS_DIR=${EM_INSTANCE_HOME}/user_projects/domains/GCDomain/servers

thisDIR=${DOMAIN_SERVERS_DIR}/EMGC_ADMINSERVER/logs
   thisAGE=7

thisFILE="GCDomain.log*"
   SweepThese
```

```
thisFILE="EMGC_ADMINSERVER.out*"
    SweepThese

thisFILE="EMGC_ADMINSERVER.log*"
    SweepThese

thisFILE="EMGC_ADMINSERVER-diagnostic-*.log"
    SweepThese

thisFILE="access.log*"
    SweepThese

# ------------------------------------------------------------------------------

EMGC_OMSn=`ls ${DOMAIN_SERVERS_DIR} | grep OMS`

thisDIR=${DOMAIN_SERVERS_DIR}/${EMGC_OMSn}/logs
    thisAGE=7

thisFILE="EMGC_OMS*.out*"
    SweepThese

for eachDIR in `ls -1 /oraoms/exportconfig`; do
    thisDIR=/oraoms/exportconfig/${eachDIR}
    thisFILE="opf_ADMIN_*.bka"
    SweepThese
Done

CleanUpFiles
exit 0
```

Section 4: EM CLI Scripting and Interactive Scripts

Release 3 of Enterprise Manager includes both the standard command-line-only version of EM CLI as well as a version with a robust scripting option (sometimes referred to as the advanced kit), which can be downloaded and installed on any supported client operating system or used directly on the server. The connection method between EM CLI and an Oracle Management Server (OMS) is the same regardless of the installation location of EM CLI. Installation instructions for the Advanced Kit are covered in Chapter 2.

The scripting option of EM CLI refers to both scripting and interactive modes. In either of these modes EM CLI expects the content of the scripts or the commands entered in interactive mode to be in Python syntax. To connect from EM CLI to Enterprise Manager in interactive mode, type the command login(username='sysman', password='foobar'). This command is a call to a Python function.

The samples in this section are the same code examples used in Chapter 6 and are all written in the Python programming language. While the samples in the previous section used the operating system shell for all of their scripting functionality (i.e., variables, for loops, if then else, etc.), the samples in this section will use EM CLI and its Jython shell for everything. Because these samples don't rely on any shell scripting functionality, they can be used on any platform supported by EM CLI.

Simple Logon Script (start.py)

The code sample below can be copied directly into a text file. It is used to set some important session properties and to establish a secure connection between the EM CLI client and the OMS to which it is connecting. Before using this script, the variables myurl, myuser, and mypass will need to be updated for your environment:

```
from emcli import *

myurl = 'https://em12cr3.example.com:7802/em'
mytrustall = 'TRUE'
myoutput = 'JSON'
myuser = 'sysman'
mypass = 'foobar'

set_client_property('EMCLI_OMS_URL', myurl)
set_client_property('EMCLI_TRUSTALL', mytrustall)
set_client_property('EMCLI_OUTPUT_TYPE', myoutput)
print(login(username=myuser, password=mypass))
```

The start.py script can be used in both scripting and interactive modes. In scripting mode, the script could be executed directly from EM CLI using the command emcli @start.py. The result would either succeed or fail in establishing a connection between EM CLI and an OMS. Using this script alone would not be very useful unless you just wanted to see the confirmation that the connection can be made.

start.py is commonly called from other scripts, or when in interactive mode, from the EM CLI Jython command-line interface (not to be confused with command-line mode). Calling start.py from another script is done by importing the script as a module.

For example, a script called sync.py is called in scripting mode with the command emcli @sync.py. Before the commands can be executed, a connection must be established between EM CLI and an OMS. If the start.py script is in a directory that is included in JYTHONPATH, the logon script can be called as the first command with import start.

■ **Note** JYTHONPATH is a shell environment variable that will be used by EM CLI to establish all of the directories to be searched when importing modules. To add a directory, supplement the variable according to the shell standards, similar to how a directory would be added to the PATH environment variable.

An alternative would be to execute the start.py in scripting mode using the command emcli @start.py and then call the sync.py (import sync) script as the last line in start.py. This method would assume that sync.py is located within the searchable path of the JYTHONPATH environment variable.

When using interactive mode, the start.py script must be in the searchable path of JYTHONPATH and be called with import start. The logon is now established for the life of the current interactive session or until the logon is implicitly (expired timeout) or explicitly (using the logout() function) dissolved.

Many Enterprise environments discourage or do not allow scripts to contain credential passwords. The start.py script can be slightly modified to take advantage of Python's capability to read external files, as shown in the next example.

Secure Logon Script (secureStart.py)

start.py has a major flaw when it comes to security, as it contains a credential password. secureStart.py, however, has the same capability as start.py to establish a connection between EM CLI and an OMS, without revealing the credential password in the script. The script instead opens a file from the filesystem that contains the password and reads the password into a variable. It then uses the contents of this variable as the credential password in the login() function.

secureStart.py is used in the same way as start.py. However, there are additional requirements. The first requirement is to create a file on a filesystem accessible from EM CLI that contains only the credential password in plain text. Secure this file with permissions appropriate for your environment. In addition to updating the myurl and the myuser script variables to match your environment, the mypassloc script variable needs to be changed to the full path location of the file containing the credential password. Take a look at the following:

```
from emcli import *

myurl = 'https://em12cr3.example.com:7802/em'
mytrustall = 'TRUE'
myoutput = 'JSON'
myuser = 'sysman'
mypassloc = '/home/oracle/.secret'

set_client_property('EMCLI_OMS_URL', myurl)
set_client_property('EMCLI_TRUSTALL', mytrustall)
set_client_property('EMCLI_OUTPUT_TYPE', myoutput)

myfile = open(mypassloc,'r')
mypass = myfile.read()

print(login(username=myuser, password=mypass))
```

The logon scripts only establish a connection between EM CLI and an OMS. They do not have any effect on the Enterprise Manager targets. The remaining samples in this section demonstrate how to manipulate targets using interactive or scripting modes.

Update Target Properties Commands (updatePropsFunc.py)

The updatePropsFunc.py script contains the commands needed to update the properties of Enterprise Manager targets. These commands can be copied individually into an EM CLI interactive session after establishing a logon. The full sample can also be put into a script and executed directly (a logon will need to be established first) with EM CLI in scripting mode using the command emcli @updatePropsFunc.py. This sample includes comments (lines beginning with the hash character) about the script commands that should be included when copying to a script. In EM CLI (as well as in Python and Jython), any line beginning with a hash character is ignored.

■ **Note**   View the logon samples at the beginning of this section for information on how to establish a logon in scripting or interactive mode.

```python
from emcli import *
import re

# Regular expression applied to target name to filter target list
# '.*' includes all targets
# '^orcl' includes all targets that begin with 'orcl'
# '^em12cr3\.example\.com$' includes target
#         with the exact name 'em12cr3.example.com'
myfiltermatch = '.*'

# Dictionary object containing the property names and values
#         to be applied to the target list
myprops = {'LifeCycle Status':'Development', 'Location':'COLO'}

# When debug is enabled, commands will be printed but not executed
debug = True

# Delimiter should be something that will not appear
#         in any target name
mydelim = '@'
mysubsep = 'property_records=' + mydelim

# Compile the target name filter
myreg = re.compile(myfiltermatch)

# Retrieve the full target list from the OMS
myobj = get_targets().out()['data']

# Loop through the full target list
for targ in myobj:
    # If the target name filter applies...
    if myreg.search(targ['Target Name']):
        myproprecs = targ['Target Name'] + mydelim + \
                     targ['Target Type'] + mydelim

        # Loop through the target properties dictionary
        #           for each target
        for propkey, propvalue in myprops.items():
            myproprecprops = propkey + mydelim + propvalue

            # If debug is True, print the command to screen
            #               without executing
            if debug:
                mycommand = 'set_target_property_value(' + \
                            'subseparator="' + mysubsep + \
                            '", property_records="' + \
                            myproprecs + \
                            myproprecprops + '")'
                print(mycommand)
```

```
# If debug is not True, print a message
#         and execute command
else:
    print('Target: ' + targ['Target Name'] + \
          ' (' + targ['Target Type'] + \
          ')\n\tProperty: ' + propkey + \
          '\n\tValue:    ' + propvalue)
    set_target_property_value(
    subseparator=mysubsep,
    property_records=myproprecs + myproprecprops)
```

Update Target Properties Class (updateProps.py)

The updateProps.py script contains a couple of import statements and a single class definition. This script does not contain any commands that are executed directly. Therefore, it would not be useful to execute this script directly (i.e., emcli @updateProps.py). The proper use would be to import the script as a module along with a logon script in interactive mode, then execute commands using the class and its functions. In scripting mode, an execution script would be created containing the commands that use the class and its functions. Import statements for updateProps.py and an import statement for a logon script would appear prior to any command executions.

To demonstrate this, create a script called changeTargProps.py. This script will be used to change target properties that use the updateProps() class. The environment in this example requires that the credential password not be contained in the executing script; therefore, the secureStart.py logon script will be used to establish a logon. The first two lines of changeTargProps.py will be import statements:

```
import secureStart
import updateProps
```

At this point in the execution of the script, there should have been a successful logon between EM CLI and the OMS, and the updateProps() class should have been imported. The rest of the commands in the script use the class functions to update the properties of a target:

```
# Create an instance of the class.
myinst = updateProps.updateProps()

# Set a single property to be applied.
myinst.props({'LifeCycle Status':'Development'})

# Include only host targets with the exact name em12cr3.example.com.
myinst.filt(namefilter='^em12cr3\.example\.com$', typefilter='^host$', show=True)

# Update the currently defined target list to the currently defined properties.
myinst.setprops(show=True)
```

This complete script could now be called in scripting mode using the command emcli @changeTargProps.py. The script would update the Lifecycle Status property of the em12cr3.example.com host target in Enterprise Manager to Development. Copying the commands from the sample into an EM CLI interactive session would have the same effect.

The functionality of updateProps() can be as simple or as complex as the situation requires. The examples below show additional methods of using updateProps(). The functionality of each example is explained using comments. Including the comments with the commands allows them to be copied with the commands into a script:

```
# Set multiple properties to be applied.
myinst.props({'LifeCycle Status':'Development', 'Location':'COLO', 'Comment':'Test EM'})

# Show the currently defined properties to be applied.
print(myinst.propdict)

# Include only host or agent targets that start with em12cr3.example.com.
myinst.filt(namefilter='^em12cr3\.example\.com', typefilter='^host|oracle_emd$')

# Include only agent targets.
myinst.filt(typefilter='^oracle_emd$')

# Include only targets managed by the em12cr3.example.com:3872 agent.
myinst.filt(agentfilter='^em12cr3\.example\.com:3872$')

# Include only host targets that start with EM, end with Service
# and have a single word between EM and Service.
myinst.filt(namefilter='^EM\s+\S+\s+Service$')

# Create an instance of the class, define the properties
# to be applied and specify the target list filters in a single command.
myinst = updateProps.updateProps(namefilter='^orcl', typefilter='oracle_dbsys',
agentfilter='em12cr3\.example\.com:3872', propdict={'LifeCycle Status':'Development'})

# Clear all filters which resets the instance to include all targets.
myinst.filt()

# Show the currently defined target list and each target's currently
# defined properties for the myinst instance.
myinst.show()

# Update the currently defined target list to the currently defined
# properties without reprinting the target and target properties list.
myinst.setprops()

# Apply a property update using the class without creating an instance.
updateProps.updateProps(
    namefilter='^orcl',
    typefilter='oracle_dbsys',
    agentfilter='em12cr3\.example\.com:3872',
    propdict={
            'LifeCycle Status':'Production',
            'Location':'DC1'}
    ).setprops(True)
```

The sample below is the updateProps.py script. The updateProps() class is heavily commented to explain the functionality of its individual components and its purpose as a whole. Additional detail about this class can be found in Chapter 6:

```
import emcli
import re
import operator

class updateProps():
    """
        The updateProps() class is used in conjuction with
        EM CLI and  allows the user to apply a defined set
        of target properties to a target list filtered at
        multiple levels with regular expressions. These
        target list filter levels include the target name,
        the target type, and the parent agent name. The
        properties can be applied to the targets using the
        class directly or using an instance of the class.

        The filtered list can be specified:
          - as class parameters and have the defined
            properties applied directly to them
          - as class parameters when creating an instance
            of the class
          - with the filt() function as part of an instance

        The defined set of target properties can specified:
          - as the class dictionary parameter 'propdict'
            and have the defined properties applied
            directly to the target list
          - as the class dictionary parameter 'propdict'
            when creating an instance of the class
          - with the props() function as part of an instance
    """
    def __init__(self, agentfilter='.*', typefilter='.*',
                namefilter='.*', propdict={}):
        self.targs = []
        self.reloadtargs = True
        self.props(propdict)
        self.__loadtargobjects()
        self.filt(agentfilter=agentfilter, typefilter=typefilter,
                namefilter=namefilter)
    def __loadtargobjects(self):
        """
        __loadtargobjects() queries the OMS for the full
        target list. The target list is then cached in the
        instance variable 'fulltargs' and each target's
        corresponding properties are assigned to the
        'targprops' instance variable. These variables
        are refreshed only when target properties have been
        applied.
```

```python
        This function is called by other functions and
        should never be called directly.
        """
    if self.reloadtargs == True:
        self.reloadtargs = False
        self.fulltargs = \
          emcli.list(resource='Targets').out()['data']
        self.targprops = \
          emcli.list(resource='TargetProperties'
                      ).out()['data']
def props(self, propdict):
    """
        props() can be called from an instance directly or
        will be called by __init__() when defining the
        instance or using the class directly. This function
        defines a dictionary object of the property names
        and values that will be applied to the defined
        target list.
    """
    assert isinstance(propdict, dict), \
            'propdict parameter must be ' + \
            'a dictionary of ' + \
             '{"property_name":"property_value"}'
    self.propdict = propdict
def filt(self, agentfilter='.*', typefilter='.*',
        namefilter='.*',
        sort=('TARGET_TYPE','TARGET_NAME'), show=False):
    """
        filt() can be called from an instance directly or
        will be called by __init__() when defining the
        instance or using the class directly. This function
        limits the target list by only including those targets
        whose properties match the defined filters.

        This function accepts the following parameters:
            agentfilter - regular expression string applied
              to the parent agent of the target
            typefilter - regular expression string applied
              to the target type value
            namefilter - regular expression string applied
              to the target name value
    """
    self.targs = []
    __agentcompfilt = re.compile(agentfilter)
    __typecompfilt = re.compile(typefilter)
    __namecompfilt = re.compile(namefilter)
    self.__loadtargobjects()
    for __inttarg in self.fulltargs:
        if __typecompfilt.search(__inttarg['TARGET_TYPE']) \
            and __namecompfilt.search(
                __inttarg['TARGET_NAME']) \
```

```python
            and (__inttarg['EMD_URL'] == None or \
            __agentcompfilt.search(__inttarg['EMD_URL'])):
                self.targs.append(__inttarg)
        __myoperator = operator
        for __myop in sort:
            __myoperator = operator.itemgetter(__myop)
        self.targssort = sorted(self.targs, key=__myoperator)
        if show == True:
            self.show()
    def show(self):
        """

        show() can be called from an instance directly or
        as a parameter from some of the other functions.
        Prints a neatly formatted display of the target name
        and type along with all of the target's currently
        defined property names and values.
        """

        print('%-5s%-40s%s' % (
            ' ', 'TARGET_TYPE'.ljust(40, '.'),
            'TARGET_NAME'))
        print('%-15s%-30s%s\n%s\n' % (
            ' ', 'PROPERTY_NAME'.ljust(30, '.'),
            'PROPERTY_VALUE', '=' * 80))
        for __inttarg in self.targssort:
            print('%-5s%-40s%s' % (
                ' ', __inttarg['TARGET_TYPE'].ljust(40, '.'),
                __inttarg['TARGET_NAME']))
            self.__showprops(__inttarg['TARGET_GUID'])
            print('')
    def __showprops(self, guid):
        """

        __showprops() prints the target properties for the
        target with the unique guid matching the 'guid'
        variable passed to the function. This function is
        called by the show() function for each target to
        print out the corresponding properties of the target.

        This function is called by other functions and
        should never be called directly.
        """

        self.__loadtargobjects()
        for __inttargprops in self.targprops:
            __intpropname = \
            __inttargprops['PROPERTY_NAME'].split('_')
            if __inttargprops['TARGET_GUID'] == guid and \
            __intpropname[0:2] == ['orcl', 'gtp']:
                print('%-15s%-30s%s' %
                    (' ', ' '.join(__intpropname[2:]).ljust(
                    30, '.'),
                    __inttargprops['PROPERTY_VALUE']))
```

161

```python
def setprops(self, show=False):
    """

        setprops() is called directly from the class or
        from an instance and calls the EM CLI function that
        applies the defined set of properties to each target
        in the filtered list of targets. The 'show' boolean
        parameter can be set to True to call the show()
        function after the properties have been applied.
    """
    assert len(self.propdict) > 0, \
            'The propdict parameter must contain ' + \
            'at least one property. Use the ' + \
            'props() function to modify.'
    self.reloadtargs = True
    __delim = '@#&@#&&'
    __subseparator = 'property_records=' + __delim
    for __inttarg in self.targs:
        for __propkey, __propvalue \
            in self.propdict.items():
            __property_records = __inttarg['TARGET_NAME'] + \
                __delim + __inttarg['TARGET_TYPE'] + \
                __delim + __propkey + __delim + __propvalue
            print('Target: ' + __inttarg['TARGET_NAME'] +
                    ' (' + __inttarg['TARGET_TYPE'] +
                    ')\n\tProperty: '
                    + __propkey + '\n\tValue: ' +
                        __propvalue + '\n')
            emcli.set_target_property_value(
                subseparator=__subseparator,
                property_records=__property_records)
    if show == True:
        self.show()
```

Index

Get the eBook for only $10!

Now you can take the weightless companion with you anywhere, anytime. Your purchase of this book entitles you to 3 electronic versions for only $10.

This Apress title will prove so indispensible that you'll want to carry it with you everywhere, which is why we are offering the eBook in 3 formats for only $10 if you have already purchased the print book.

Convenient and fully searchable, the PDF version enables you to easily find and copy code—or perform examples by quickly toggling between instructions and applications. The MOBI format is ideal for your Kindle, while the ePUB can be utilized on a variety of mobile devices.

Go to www.apress.com/promo/tendollars to purchase your companion eBook.

Apress®
THE EXPERT'S VOICE™